Connect to Text

Strategies for Close Reading and Writing

Author
Jessica Hathaway, M.S.Ed.

SHELL EDUCATION

Publishing Credits

Corinne Burton, M.A.Ed., *President*; Kimberly Stockton, M.A.Ed, *Vice President of Education*; Sara Johnson, M.S.Ed., *Content Director*; Kristy Stark, M.A.Ed., *Editor*; Courtney Patterson, *Multimedia Designer*; Marissa Dunham, *Editorial Assistant*

Image Credits

p.47: Getty Images; p.110: Dreamstime; all other images Shutterstock

Standards

© 2010. National Governors Association Center for Best Practices and Council of Chief State School Officers. All rights reserved.

Shell Education

5301 Oceanus Drive
Huntington Beach, CA 92649-1030
http://www.shelleducation.com

ISBN 978-1-4258-1505-9

© 2015 Shell Educational Publishing, Inc.

Table of Contents

Appendices

Introduction

In the continually changing world of education, it is common to have shifts in policies, practices, and areas of emphasis. With job requirements becoming increasingly demanding and more students pursuing college degrees, there is now a greater emphasis on college and career readiness in US public schools. In many states, this shift came with the adoption of the Common Core State Standards (CCSS). These standards were designed to outline the skills and knowledge necessary for students to "succeed in college, career, and life, regardless of where they live" (NGA and CCSSO 2010b). Even states that have not formally adopted the CCSS face mounting pressure to prepare students more rigorously for the complex demands of life after high school. As a result of these increasing demands and higher expectations, recent history has seen numerous changes in both educational objectives and classroom teaching practices.

Key Shifts in Standards and Instructional Objectives

Within the domain of English language arts and literacy, the CCSS and many other state standards dictate several major shifts from previous practices. These shifts address the balance between informational and literary texts, the use of literacy instruction in the content areas, and the importance of reading increasingly complex texts. These changes also specify the need for text-based answers in both written work and classroom discussions. Additionally, today's standards emphasize supporting responses with textual evidence, and they stress the significance of building academic vocabularies of associated, relevant words.

Emphasis on Informational Text

Traditionally, elementary literacy instruction focused primarily on narratives and other literary texts. Given the importance of informational texts in our daily lives, revised literacy curricula now focus more heavily on informational texts. According to Maloch and Bomer (2013), "Children write what they read. If they read (and hear) lots and lots of stories, they are better at composing stories. If, on the other hand, they read (and hear) stories, but also informational books, procedural texts, and feature articles, they are more likely to learn the conventions of those genres and be able to compose according to those purposes" (206).

Rather than concentrating on narrative texts in the primary years and then suddenly expecting students to be able to read and write informational texts by middle school, the new format for literacy instruction mandates a balance between literature and informational texts starting in kindergarten. According to the National Assessment Governing Board (2008), at least 50 percent of elementary students' reading should be informational text every year. In the middle school years, this balance shifts to 45 percent literary and 55 percent informational texts, and by high school, students should read 30 percent literary and 70 percent informational texts.

Building Knowledge and Literacy in the Content Areas

The view of reading as an isolated subject that should be taught only in language arts classes has also shifted. Now, all teachers, including those in content areas, such as science and social studies, are encouraged to integrate literacy into their curriculums. In the content areas, students are no longer just reading to learn; they are also learning to read. Content-area teachers help their students learn *about* texts, as well as from them. Elder and Paul (2014) point out that students need to develop the ability to understand text structure in order to access the information in a science or social studies textbook. Once students have a general understanding of the structure of a textbook, they are more able to learn information from the text, ask and answer questions about the information, and use the textbook as a resource for future learning.

The content areas can also expose students to a wide variety of texts. In social studies classes, for example, students read primary sources, including letters, interviews, and diary entries, produced by people who witnessed or participated in the events being studied. In order to comprehend these, students must take many different elements into consideration. For instance, the students must consider the type of source, the context or setting in which the text was produced, the perspective of the author or creator, and the reliability of the source (Morgan and Rasinski 2012). By teaching the reading skills necessary to access primary sources, teachers help students improve their critical-thinking skills and knowledge of the subject matter (Veccia 2004).

Complex Texts

While it may seem obvious that students need to be able to read complex texts for college and career readiness, the details of how to help students achieve this goal are less clear. College textbooks and workplace documents often include challenging vocabulary, complex ideas, and intricate text structures. In order to be able to comprehend these texts, students must have the skills and strategies to access the information in the text. They must be comfortable confronting complicated texts that require multiple readings. They must also have practice persevering, even when frustrated. These are daunting tasks for students of all ages and only through a concerted effort on the part of teachers, parents, schools, and administrators will students be successful. Through careful text selection, diligent instruction, and appropriate scaffolding, students can learn how to approach complex texts with confidence.

Text Connections

While reading and writing have always been closely linked, there is now an increased emphasis on the direct, explicit connection between reading, writing, and discussing text.

In support of current standards, students are encouraged to read texts multiple times and refer to them explicitly in classroom discussions. They must support written and verbal responses with evidence from the text. Rather than simply decoding and comprehending text, students must also analyze text in order to form their own opinions and judgments about the reasoning and evidence presented. Classroom teachers should offer opportunities for students to explore texts through in-depth discussions. During these discussions, teachers must remind students to support their ideas with text-based information.

Evidence-Based Writing

Just as the emphasis in reading has shifted to include more informational text, so has the focus of writing in today's standards. Historically, most elementary writing assignments asked students to compose narratives based on their own experiences and opinions. While narrative writing is still part of the standards, it is no longer the sole focus. Students are now expected to write informational texts and arguments. The 2011 Writing Framework created by the National Assessment Governing Board specifies that the purpose of writing tasks for fourth-grade students should be fairly evenly distributed between argument writing (30 percent), explanatory writing (35 percent), and narrative writing (35 percent). By eighth grade, the distribution should shift to 35 percent argument writing, 35 percent explanatory writing, and 30 percent narrative writing. The focus on informational writing continues to increase as students mature. By twelfth grade, only 20 percent of students' writing should be based on personal experiences, while the other 80 percent should be evenly split between explanatory and argument writing (National Assessment Governing Board 2007).

Along with an increased emphasis on informational and argument writing comes a greater focus on text-based evidence. Just as students are expected to provide text-based support for their oral arguments, they are also expected to base their written works on information and evidence from texts. As students' writing capabilities grow, they should be able to compile information from multiple sources to write compelling arguments and detailed explanatory texts. These types of writing skills become especially important as students enter college classes and careers where the ability to analyze, inform, convince, and persuade through writing is necessary.

Vocabulary

Being college and career ready in today's world also means having a rich, academic vocabulary. This shift focuses on the types of words students learn, rather than the amount of words. Teachers must build students' vocabularies with relevant, transferable words that will enable them to access complex texts (Wilfong 2013). Teachers must eliminate arcane words that have little use beyond a particular project or text, and focus instead on teaching words that are essential for comprehension and content knowledge. Teachers can make these new words even more meaningful for students by associating them with familiar words (McKeown et al. 2013).

Close Reading

Close reading is the careful reading of a text, often multiple times, to obtain a deeper understanding of its meaning (Brown and Kappes 2012). According to the Partnership for Assessment of Readiness for College and Careers,

> Close, analytic reading stresses engaging with a text of sufficient complexity directly and examining its meaning thoroughly and methodically, encouraging students to read and reread deliberately. Directing student attention on the text itself empowers students to understand the central ideas and key supporting details. It also enables students to reflect on the meanings of individual words and sentences; the order in which sentences unfold; and the development of ideas over the course of the text, which ultimately leads students to arrive at an understanding of the text as a whole. (PARCC 2015, para. 15)

Close reading is not a new concept. High school and college courses have always required students to analyze texts. However, many students found themselves facing those expectations without the skills necessary for the types of methodical, analytical reading that was required (Brown and Kappes 2012). Today's standards highlight the importance of explicitly teaching close reading skills beginning even in kindergarten.

Close reading may be performed in a variety of different ways, but several key characteristics generally set this type of instruction apart from other instructional practices. According to Burke (2013), close reading is comprised of the following elements:

- short passages of complex text
- limited pre-reading activities
- multiple readings of the text
- analytical discussions
- text-dependent questions

Short Passages of Complex Text

So what does close reading instruction look like in the classroom? Before beginning any close reading lesson, the teacher must first select the text. The selected text should be relatively short to allow for multiple readings of the same passage. In the lower grades, a paragraph or two is adequate and, by high school, close reading passages may be up to several pages long.

#51505—Connect to Text: Strategies for Close Reading and Writing

© Shell Education

The selected text must also be challenging and complex. The text should include sufficient complexity to keep the students engaged over the course of several readings. Students should be encouraged to struggle with the text during close reading. Teachers should consider "age appropriateness of the text and likely interest of the students, complexity of ideas, text and sentence structure, vocabulary difficulty, and length of the text" when selecting a text for close reading (Jones et al. 2014, 6). The ideal text for close reading has multiple literary elements and layers of intricacy. For example, a text passage that contains a detailed description of the setting, a unique text structure, and several interesting visual elements would provide both the teacher and the students with several different topics for close reading activities.

Limited Pre-Reading Activities

While background knowledge always plays a role in the comprehension of any text, the goal of close reading is to analyze and interpret the information directly presented in the text while limiting the confounding influence of personal experience. As a result, teachers are encouraged to limit pre-reading activities and instead teach the students the skills necessary to comprehend the text independently (Conklin and Murphy 2014; Fisher, Frey, and Lapp 2012). Teachers may choose to teach or review several important vocabulary words that will enable students to access the text, but aside from that, students immediately engage with the text through an initial first reading experience without additional prompting or preparation.

Multiple Readings of the Text

After the teacher has selected a sufficiently short and complex text, students are ready to begin reading. Depending on the age and reading abilities of the students, the first reading of the text may take the form of a choral, group, partner, or independent reading experience. Younger students will probably benefit from hearing the text read aloud for the first reading, while older students are often capable of reading the text independently. The objective of the first reading is to gather initial impressions of the text, identify areas of confusion, ask questions about the text, and note key concepts or text features. Students should be encouraged to annotate the text as they read or listen to it. They should be instructed to underline or circle confusing words or phrases, write questions in the margins, draw arrows to indicate connections between ideas, and note any sentences or topics that they would like to explore in greater depth. At first, students will need to have these annotation skills modeled. Many teachers use a projector or document camera to demonstrate these techniques to the class. Eventually, however, students should be able to record their initial impressions independently during the first reading of the text. Next, the teacher should ask students to share their thoughts about the text and use these ideas and identified areas of confusion to guide subsequent readings of the text.

After the initial reading of the text, students engage in a variety of activities to help them delve deeper into the text. Throughout the discussion and classroom activity, the teacher and students refer back to the text for specific information to support their ideas.

A close reading lesson usually includes two or three re-readings of the same text. For each reading, students are asked to focus on a different aspect of the text. The CCSS Anchor Standards for Reading break down text analysis into three categories: key ideas and details, craft and structure, and integration of knowledge and ideas. When designing your own close reading lessons, it may be helpful to include one activity for each category. For example, students might read the first time to determine the main idea. The second reading might focus on using text features to find information. The third reading might ask students to integrate information from the illustrations and the words in the text.

Analytical Discussions

Analytical classroom discussions are a significant part of any close reading instruction. Oftentimes, close reading is presented as a replacement for the rambling, unfocused classroom discussions that sometimes characterize language arts lessons. However, rather than being opposed, analytical reading and classroom discussions are actually both integral parts of effective close reading instruction. Snow and O'Connor (2013) write that, "close reading and discussion can form symbiotic relationships with tremendous potential for learning" (7). However, they also point out that both close reading and classroom discussions can be challenging and necessitate adequate support and organization for both teachers and students. In order to hold successful classroom discussions, teachers must lay a solid foundation of general discussion guidelines and be prepared to provide prompts and feedback to facilitate the discussion. As part of an integrated literacy experience, discussions about the text provide the ideal platform for students to share the discoveries they made during close reading. Furthermore, these discussions allow students to build on each other's ideas, explore the connections between concepts, and review how these new ideas relate to the overall meaning of the text passage. During the discussions, teachers need to be prepared to facilitate the direction and content and to ensure that the students' contributions are directly related to the text. By encouraging students to support their ideas with evidence from the text, teachers keep discussions focused and productive (Fisher and Frey 2014).

Text-Dependent Questions

Text-dependent questions enable students to dig deeper into texts and explore various facets of content and text structure. Text-dependent questions are questions that relate directly to the text. Their answers do not depend on background knowledge or personal experience. There are many types of text-dependent questions, and effective text-dependent questions go beyond simply asking students to recall details from the text. Text-dependent questions should guide students in a thorough, in-depth examination of the text "to enhance learning, engage students' critical-thinking skills, and increase comprehension" (Hathaway 2014, 7).

These questions should be tailored to fit the area of focus for each section of a close reading lesson. For example, to guide students' analysis of an author's argument, you might ask the following text-dependent questions:

- *What main points is the author making?*

- *Which claims are supported by reasons? Which are not?*

- *What evidence did the author give to support the main point that _____? Was the source of the evidence credible?*

There are three main categories of text-dependent questions that correspond to the three categories of CCSS Anchor Standards for Reading (Jones et al. 2014). Questions about key ideas and details focus on *what the text says*, questions about craft and structure address *how the text says it*, and questions about the integration of knowledge and ideas show *what it means*. For example, a question that helps students see the cause-and-effect structure of a text teaches the students *how* the author uses structure to explain relationships among ideas.

Teachers can use text-dependent questions to stimulate discussion, assess comprehension, or as writing prompts. These types of questions should be integrated throughout the close reading lesson and used to help the students focus on the text explicitly. When answering or discussing a text-dependent question, either verbally or in writing, students should be required to include evidence and information directly from the text to support their answers, opinions, and ideas. If necessary, teachers must redirect students' focus so that it remains centered on the text throughout the lesson.

When Should Close Reading Be Used?

Close reading is a specific instructional practice that should be part of a well-balanced curriculum in language arts and the content areas (Brown and Kappes 2012). In addition to close reading, students should also engage in broad text-based discussions, collaborative projects, related writing assignments, and much more. Teachers should use close reading lessons to examine small sections of text to achieve specific educational goals. For instance, close reading is an effective tool for exploring content, text structure, vocabulary, literary elements, and arguments presented in texts. However, close reading activities should be used to complement, rather than replace, existing reading practices in the classroom, such as guided reading groups and traditional classroom discussions (Fisher and Frey 2014).

Why Should Close Reading Be Used?

If close reading is not a new practice, and it represents only one part of a well-balanced curriculum, why is it receiving so much attention these days? The answer is that close reading is an effective tool for helping students meet the rigorous, new reading standards. For students and teachers who find the increased emphasis on informational text intimidating, close reading helps break down the process of analyzing texts. It also provides an excellent guide for content-area teachers to incorporate literacy instruction into the curriculum, while at the same time helping students better comprehend their reading assignments. Close reading helps students access complex texts and practice new strategies for comprehending them (Conklin and Murphy 2014). Additionally, close reading activities train students to reference texts for evidence and support. Through close reading, students also gain the in-depth knowledge required to complete evidence-based writing projects. Finally, close reading is an excellent mechanism for learning new vocabulary, studying the associations between words, building connections among concepts, and examining the effect of word choice on meaning. When used effectively, close reading can help teachers make the instructional changes mandated by the new educational expectations.

Connecting Close Reading and Writing

Reading and writing have always been closely connected in the language arts curriculum. So how does close reading change this relationship? Close reading can improve writing in two important ways: as a means to access the content of a text and as a way to explore a text as a model.

First and foremost, close reading helps students access the content of a text and provides them with material for their writing. For example, a close reading of a biology text might clarify the relationship between photosynthesis and respiration in plants. A student could use this information to write an explanatory text about plant functions. This type of close reading is also helpful in argument writing, especially when responding to an argument or claim. For example, after reading an opinion piece in favor of school uniforms, a student might write an argument against school uniforms. In order to write a convincing argument, the student must identify the opposing views and counter these arguments. Close reading is a tool for gathering information, ideas, and arguments that students can use in their own writing.

In addition to helping students comprehend a text so that they can use it as a resource in their writing, close reading also enables students to use a text as a mentor text. A mentor text is a text that is used as a model for the student's own writing. In the words of Gallagher (2014), "If we want our students to write persuasive arguments, interesting explanatory pieces, or captivating narratives, we need to have them read, analyze, and emulate persuasive arguments, interesting explanatory pieces, and captivating narratives" (29). Through reading, comprehending, and imitating selected texts, students can learn a wide variety of skills to apply to their own writing. Close reading is the key that helps students elucidate the complicated text structures, creative styles of narration, interwoven themes, complex figurative language, and other important literary components in mentor texts. In other words, close reading techniques serve as scaffolds that enable students to improve their own writing through mentor texts.

How to Use This Book

This book has four sections:
- strategies for close reading and writing
- close reading lessons with informational/explanatory texts
- close reading lessons with opinion/argument texts
- close reading lessons with narrative texts

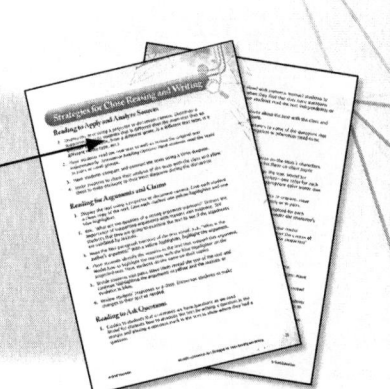

The first section provides general **strategies for close reading and writing**. These strategies can be used when working with any text to create new lessons for close reading and writing.

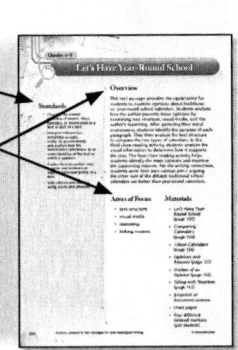

Each lesson begins with a list of **standards** that are addressed. The specific **areas of focus** and **materials** are listed after the overview in each lesson.

The **overview** discusses the type of text used in the lesson and the ways in which the standards connect to the text passage. The overview also provides a brief description of the reading and writing activities in the lesson.

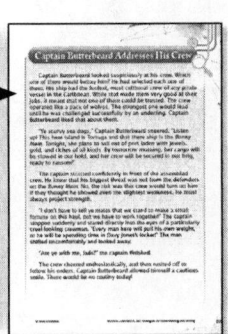

Each lesson contains a **text** that is appropriate for the grade span. A variety of text types are in this resource. Be sure to make at least one copy of the text for each student. It may also be helpful to display the text using a projector or document camera. For shorter texts, you may choose to rewrite the text on chart paper so that class can annotate it together.

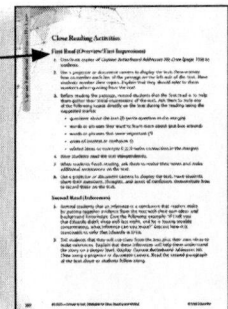

The lessons begin with a **first reading** of the text, where students give their initial impressions, thoughts, and questions about the text. The teacher prompts students to record notes about specific aspects of the text, such as words they find confusing, or concepts they think are related to the text. Students record these notes directly on the text.

The procedure for the **second, third, and fourth readings** vary greatly, depending on the text and areas of focus. Before beginning the lesson, teachers should informally assess their students' knowledge and skills so that they can tailor the lesson to fit the needs of their students. All of the reading activities are self-contained and may be taught in any order. It is not necessary to complete all four reading activities, so teachers may choose those that are most relevant to their students' instructional needs.

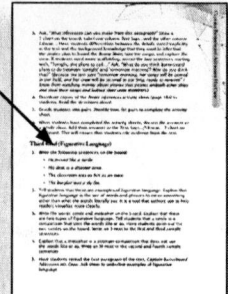

Each lesson finishes with a **culminating writing activity**. Students produce a piece of writing that matches the type of text in the lesson (informational, argument, or narrative). These writing tasks require students to apply the knowledge and skills they acquired through the close reading activities. Some writing activities focus on the use of the text as a resource. In other writing activities, students use the text passage as a mentor text.

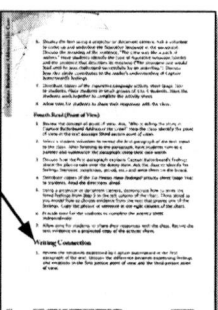

Student activity sheets support students during the close reading and writing activities.

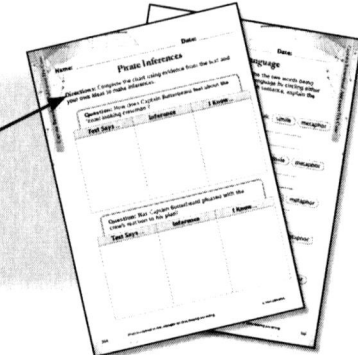

Correlation to Standards

Shell Education is committed to producing educational materials that are research- and standards-based. In this effort, we have correlated all of our products to the academic standards of all 50 United States, the District of Columbia, the Department of Defense Dependent Schools, and all Canadian provinces. We have also correlated to the Common Core State Standards.

How to Find Standards Correlations

To print a customized correlation report of this product for your state, visit our website at **http://www.shelleducation.com** and follow the on-screen directions. If you require assistance in printing correlation reports, please contact Customer Service at 1-877-777-3450.

Purpose and Intent of Standards

Legislation mandates that all states adopt academic standards that identify the skills students will learn in kindergarten through grade twelve. Many states also have standards for Pre-K. This same legislation sets requirements to ensure the standards are detailed and comprehensive.

Standards are designed to focus instruction and guide adoption of curricula. Standards are statements that describe the criteria necessary for students to meet specific academic goals. They define the knowledge, skills, and content students should acquire at each level. Standards are also used to develop standardized tests to evaluate students' academic progress. Teachers are required to demonstrate how their lessons meet state standards. State standards are used in the development of all of our products, so educators can be assured they meet the academic requirements of each state.

Common Core State Standards

The lessons in this book are aligned to the Common Core State Standards (CCSS). The standards provided on the Digital Resource CD (standards.pdf) support the objectives presented throughout the lessons.

TESOL and WIDA Standards

The lessons in this book promote English language development for English language learners. The standards listed on the Digital Resource CD (standards.pdf) support the language objectives.

Grade	Standard	Lesson
Kindergarten	**RL.K.1**—With prompting and support, ask and answer questions about key details in a text	At the Beach (page 139)
	RL.K.5—Recognize common types of texts	At the Beach (page 139)
	RL.K.7—With prompting and support, describe the relationship between illustrations and the story in which they appear	At the Beach (page 139)
	RI.K.1—With prompting and support, ask and answer questions about key details in a text	I Can Work (page 38)
	RI.K.3—With prompting and support, describe the connection between two individuals, events, ideas, or pieces of information in a text	I Can Work (page 38)
	RI.K.7—With prompting and support, describe the relationship between illustrations and the text in which they appear (e.g., what person, place, thing, or idea in the text an illustration depicts)	I Can Work (page 38)
	W.K.2—Use a combination of drawing, dictating, and writing to compose informative/explanatory texts in which they name what they are writing about and supply some information about the topic	I Can Work (page 38)
	W.K.3—Use a combination of drawing, dictating, and writing to narrate a single event or several loosely linked events, tell about the events in the order in which they occurred, and provide a reaction to what happened	At the Beach (page 139)
First Grade	**RI.1.1**—Ask and answer questions about key details in a text	The Best Job (page 85)
	RI.1.3—Describe the connection between two individuals, events, ideas, or pieces of information in a text	The Best Job (page 85)
	RI.1.8—Identify the reasons an author gives to support points in a text	The Best Job (page 85)
	W.1.1—Write opinion pieces in which they introduce the topic or name the book they are writing about, state an opinion, supply a reason for the opinion, and provide some sense of closure	The Best Job (page 85)
Second Grade	**RL.2.2**—Recount stories, including fables and folktales from diverse cultures, and determine their central message, lesson, or moral	Why the Chipmunk Has Black Stripes (page 148)
	RL.2.3—Describe how characters in a story respond to major events and challenges	Why the Chipmunk Has Black Stripes (page 148)
	RL.2.6—Acknowledge differences in the points of view of characters, including by speaking in a different voice for each character when reading dialogue aloud	Why the Chipmunk Has Black Stripes (page 148)
	W.2.3—Write narratives in which they recount a well-elaborated event or short sequence of events, include details to describe actions, thoughts, and feelings, use temporal words to signal event order, and provide a sense of closure	Why the Chipmunk Has Black Stripes (page 148)

Grade	Standard	Lesson
Third Grade	**RI.3.1**—Ask and answer questions to demonstrate understanding of a text, referring explicitly to the text as the basis for the answers	The Birthday Wish (page 94)
	RI.3.2—Determine the main idea of a text; recount the key details and explain how they support the main idea	Choices (page 46)
	RI.3.4—Determine the meaning of general academic and domain-specific words and phrases in a text relevant to a grade 3 topic or subject area	Choices (page 46)
	RI.3.6—Distinguish their own point of view from that of the author of a text	The Birthday Wish (page 94)
	RI.3.7—Use information gained from illustrations and the words in a text to demonstrate understanding of the text	Choices (page 46)
	RI.3.8—Describe the logical connection between particular sentences and paragraphs in a text	The Birthday Wish (page 94)
	W.3.1.A—Introduce the topic or text they are writing about, state an opinion, and create an organizational structure that lists reasons	The Birthday Wish (page 94)
	W.3.2—Introduce a topic and group related information together; include illustrations when useful to aiding comprehension	Choices (page 46)
Fourth Grade	**RI.4.5**—Describe the overall structure of events, ideas, concepts, or information in a text or part of a text	Let's Have Year-Round School (page 104)
	RI.4.7—Interpret information presented visually, orally, or quantitatively and explain how the information contributes to an understanding of the text in which it appears	Let's Have Year-Round School (page 104)
	RI.4.8—Explain how an author uses reasons and evidence to support particular points in a text	Let's Have Year-Round School (page 104)
	W.4.1.C—Link opinion and reasons using words and phrases	Let's Have Year-Round School (page 104)
Fifth Grade	**RL.5.1**—Quote accurately from a text when explaining what the text says explicitly and when drawing inferences from the text	Captain Butterbeard Addresses His Crew (page 158)
	RL.5.4—Determine the meaning of words and phrases as they are used in a text, including figurative language such as metaphors and similes	Captain Butterbeard Addresses His Crew (page 158)
	RL.5.6—Describe how a narrator's or speaker's point of view influences how events are described	Captain Butterbeard Addresses His Crew (page 158)
	RI.5.3—Explain the relationships or interactions between two or more individuals, events, ideas, or concepts in a historical, scientific, or technical text based on specific information in the text	Ordering Whole Numbers (page 53)
	RI.5.4—Determine the meaning of general academic and domain-specific words and phrases in a text relevant to a grade 5 topic or subject area	Ordering Whole Numbers (page 53)
	RI.5.5—Compare and contrast the overall structure of events, ideas, concepts, or information in two or more texts	Ordering Whole Numbers (page 53)
	RI.5.7—Draw on information from multiple print or digital sources, demonstrating the ability to locate an answer to a question quickly or to solve a problem efficiently	Ordering Whole Numbers (page 53)
	W.5.2.D—Use precise language and domain-specific vocabulary to inform about or explain the topic	Ordering Whole Numbers (page 53)
	W.5.3.B—Use narrative techniques, such as dialogue, description, and pacing, to develop experiences and events or show the responses of characters to situations	Captain Butterbeard Addresses His Crew (page 158)

Grade	Standard	Lesson
Sixth Grade	**RL.6.4**—Determine the meaning of words and phrases as they are used in a text, including figurative and connotative meanings; analyze the impact of a specific word choice on meaning and tone	A Midsummer Night's Dream, Act II Scene I (page 168)
Sixth Grade	**RL.6.5**—Analyze how a particular sentence, chapter, scene, or stanza fits into the overall structure of a text and contributes to the development of the theme, setting, or plot	A Midsummer Night's Dream, Act II Scene I (page 168)
Sixth Grade	**RL.6.7**—Compare and contrast the experience of reading a story, drama, or poem to listening to or viewing an audio, video, or live version of the text, including contrasting what they "see" and "hear" when reading the text to what they perceive when they listen or watch	A Midsummer Night's Dream, Act II Scene I (page 168)
Sixth Grade	**RI.6.3**—Analyze in detail how a key individual, event, or idea is introduced, illustrated, and elaborated in a text (e.g., through examples or anecdotes)	Hatshepsut: The Female Pharaoh (page 62)
Sixth Grade	**RI.6.5**—Analyze how a particular sentence, paragraph, chapter, or section fits into the overall structure of a text and contributes to the development of the ideas	Hatshepsut: The Female Pharaoh (page 62)
Sixth Grade	**RI.6.6**—Determine an author's point of view or purpose in a text and explain how it is conveyed in the text	Hatshepsut: The Female Pharaoh (page 62)
Sixth Grade	**W.6.2.A**—Introduce a topic; organize ideas, concepts, and information, using strategies such as definition, classification, comparison/contrast, and cause/effect; include formatting (e.g., headings), graphics (e.g., charts, tables), and multimedia when useful to aiding comprehension	Hatshepsut: The Female Pharaoh (page 62)
Sixth Grade	**W.6.3.B**—Use narrative techniques, such as dialogue, pacing, and description, to develop experiences, events, and/or characters	A Midsummer Night's Dream, Act II Scene I (page 168)
Seventh Grade	**RI.7.2**—Determine two or more central ideas in a text and analyze their development over the course of the text; provide an objective summary of the text	Saving Our National Parks (page 114)
Seventh Grade	**RI.7.4**—Determine the meaning of words and phrases as they are used in a text, including figurative, connotative, and technical meanings; analyze the impact of a specific word choice on meaning and tone	Saving Our National Parks (page 114)
Seventh Grade	**RI.7.8**—Trace and evaluate the argument and specific claims in a text, assessing whether the reasoning is sound and the evidence is relevant and sufficient to support the claims	Saving Our National Parks (page 114)
Seventh Grade	**W.7.1.B**—Support claim(s) with clear reasons and relevant evidence, using accurate, credible sources and demonstrating an understanding of the topic or text	Saving Our National Parks (page 114)
Ninth to Tenth Grade	**RI.9–10.3**—Analyze how the author unfolds an analysis or series of ideas or events, including the order in which the points are made, how they are introduced and developed, and the connections that are drawn between them.	Flag Day Address June 14, 1917 (page 124)
Ninth to Tenth Grade	**RI.9–10.8**—Delineate and evaluate the argument and specific claims in a text, assessing whether the reasoning is valid and the evidence is relevant and sufficient; identify false statements and fallacious reasoning	Flag Day Address June 14, 1917 (page 124)
Ninth to Tenth Grade	**RI.9–10.9**—Analyze seminal US documents of historical and literary significance, including how they address related themes and concepts	Flag Day Address June 14, 1917 (page 124)
Ninth to Tenth Grade	**W.9–10.1.A**—Introduce precise claim(s), distinguish the claim(s) from alternate or opposing claims, and create an organization that establishes clear relationships among claim(s), counterclaims, reasons, and evidence	Flag Day Address June 14, 1917 (page 124)

Grade	Standard	Lesson
Eleventh to Twelfth Grade	**RL.11–12.1**—Cite strong and thorough textual evidence to support analysis of what the text says explicitly as well as inferences drawn from the text, including determining where the text leaves matters uncertain	The Legend of Sleepy Hollow (page 177)
	RL.11–12.3—Analyze the impact of the author's choices regarding how to develop and relate elements of a story or drama	The Legend of Sleepy Hollow (page 177)
	RL.11–12.4—Determine the meaning of words and phrases as they are used in the text, including figurative and connotative meanings; analyze the impact of specific word choices on meaning and tone, including words with multiple meanings or language that is particularly fresh, engaging, or beautiful	The Legend of Sleepy Hollow (page 177)
	RI.11–12.1—Cite strong and thorough textual evidence to support analysis of what the text says explicitly as well as inferences drawn from the text, including determining where the text leaves matters uncertain	The United States Bill of Rights (page 72)
	RI.11–12.2—Determine two or more central ideas of a text and analyze their development over the course of the text, including how they interact and build on one another to provide a complex analysis; provide an objective summary of the text	The United States Bill of Rights (page 72)
	RI.11–12.4—Determine the meaning of words and phrases as they are used in a text, including figurative, connotative, and technical meanings; analyze how an author uses and refines the meaning of a key term or terms over the course of a text	The United States Bill of Rights (page 72)
	RI.11–12.9—Analyze seventeenth-, eighteenth-, and nineteenth-century foundational US documents of historical and literary significance for their themes, purposes, and rhetorical features	The United States Bill of Rights (page 72)
	W.11–12.2.B—Develop the topic thoroughly by selecting the most significant and relevant facts, extended definitions, concrete details, quotations, or other information and examples appropriate to the audience's knowledge of the topic	The United States Bill of Rights (page 72)
	W.11–12.3.D—Use precise words and phrases, telling details, and sensory language to convey a vivid picture of the experiences, events, setting, and/or characters	The Legend of Sleepy Hollow (page 177)

TESOL Standards

Standard	Lesson
Standard 1: English language learners communicate for social, intercultural, and instructional purposes within the school setting.	All lessons
Standard 2: English language learners communicate information, ideas, and concepts necessary for academic success in the area of language arts.	All lessons

WIDA Standards

Standard	Lesson
Standard 1: English language learners communicate for social, intercultural, and instructional purposes within the school setting.	All lessons
Standard 2: English language learners communicate information, ideas, and concepts necessary for academic success in the area of language arts.	All lessons

Strategies for Close Reading and Writing

These strategies are embedded throughout the lessons within this book. They can also be used when working with texts outside of what is provided in this book.

Reading to Apply and Analyze Sources

1. Display the text using a projector or document camera. Distribute a supporting text to students that is different than the main text (has an alternate perspective, from a different genre, is a different text type, is a different media type, etc.).

2. Have students read the new text as well as reread the original text independently. Alternative Reading Options: Have students read the texts in pairs or small groups.

3. Have students compare and contrast the texts using a Venn diagram.

4. Invite students to share their analysis of the texts with the class and allow them to make revisions to their Venn diagrams during the discussion.

Reading for Arguments and Claims

1. Display the text using a projector or document camera. Give each student a clean copy of the text. Give each student one yellow highlighter and one blue highlighter.

2. Ask, "What are the qualities of a strong argument (opinion)?" Discuss the importance of supporting arguments with reasons and evidence. Tell students that they are going to examine the text to see if the arguments are validated by reasons.

3. Read the first paragraph (section) of the text aloud. Ask, "What is the author's argument?" With a yellow highlighter, highlight the argument.

4. Have students identify the reasons in the text that support this argument. Model how to highlight the reasons with the blue highlighter on the projected text. Have students do the same on their copies.

5. Divide students into pairs. Have them reread the rest of the text and continue highlighting the arguments in yellow and the reasons or evidence in blue.

6. Review students' responses as a class. Encourage students to make changes to their text as needed.

Reading to Ask Questions

1. Explain to students that sometimes we have questions as we read. Model for students how to annotate the text by writing a question in the margin and placing a question mark in the text to show where they had a question.

2. Have students reread the text aloud with partners. Instruct students to annotate the text as they read when they find that they have questions. Alternative Reading Options: Have students read the text independently or chorally as a class.

3. Allow students to share their questions about the text with the class and record them on a chart or on the board.

4. Discuss whether the text provides answers to some of the questions that were posed, or whether further investigation or inferences need to be made in order to find an answer.

Reading for Characters

1. Tell students that with this read they will focus on the story's characters. Ask students to name the characters as you list them on chart paper.

2. Use a projector or document camera to display the text. Model for students how to code the story with different colors—one color for each character. Students should highlight with the appropriate color words that describe each different character.

3. Provide each student with different colored markers or crayons. Have students code the text as they reread it independently or in pairs.

4. Have students share the words or phrases they highlighted for each character and record their words on the chart paper under the character's name.

5. As a class, discuss how the words used in the text help the reader understand the characters (how the characters change over the course of the text, how the characters are described visually, how the characters' emotions are conveyed, etc.).

Reading to Connect Information

1. Display a copy of the text using a projector or document camera.

2. Have students reread the text chorally. Alternative Reading Options: Have students read the text independently or in pairs.

3. Select two sentences that have a connection (e.g., description) and reread them aloud to the class.

4. Ask, "What is the connection between these two sentences?" Help students understand the connection. Draw an arrow between the two sentences to show the connection.

5. Repeat Steps 3 and 4 to show another example of a connection in the text.

6. Have students work in pairs or independently to draw arrows between other connections in the text.

7. Invite students to share their connections and record their thoughts on the displayed text. Allow students to make additional arrows and/or notes as others share.

Reading for Explicit vs. Implied Information

1. To review the difference between explicitly stated information and implied information, write the following sentence on the board: When Martin walked into the room, he stopped suddenly in his tracks and screamed. Ask, "What details are stated explicitly in this sentence?" (*Martin walked into a room; Martin stopped suddenly; Martin screamed.*) Ask, "What can you infer from the sentence?" (*Martin saw something that surprised him.*) Then ask, "What is left uncertain in this sentence?" (*Is he scared or happy or excited? Is he in trouble? Does he need help?*)

2. Explain that it is important to differentiate between information that is presented explicitly, inferences made from the text, and places where the text leaves matters uncertain.

3. Have a volunteer read a portion of the text aloud. Model how to annotate the text to indicate which information is explicit, implied, and uncertain.

4. Place students in pairs and have them reread the text together. In pairs, allow them time to annotate the text to find explicitly stated information, implied information, and areas of uncertainty. Ask students to annotate their text accordingly.

5. Provide time for pairs to share their responses with the class.

Reading for Figurative Language

1. Write the following sentences on the board:

   • The cheetah ran like the wind.

   • Her room is a disaster area.

   • I am so full, I could explode!

   • The thunder roared so loud I could hardly hear myself think.

   • I could tell that he got up on the wrong side of the bed.

2. Tell students that these are examples of figurative language. Explain that figurative language is the use of words and phrases to mean something other than what the words literally say. It is a tool that authors use to help readers visualize a comparison or an idea more clearly.

3. Write the words simile, metaphor, hyperbole, personification, and idiom on the board. Explain that these are five types of figurative language.

4. Explain the meaning of each type of figurative language and decide as a class which example belongs with which type. (*The cheetah ran like the wind—simile; Her room is a disaster area—metaphor; I am so full, I could explode!—hyperbole; The thunder roared so loud I could hardly hear myself think—personification; I could tell that he got up on the wrong side of the bed—idiom.*)

5. Have students reread the text independently and ask them to underline examples of figurative language.

6. Display the text using a projector or document camera. Ask a volunteer to come up and underline the figurative language in the text and identify what type of figurative language is used.

7. Model for students how to make a note in the margin about the type of figurative language and what the figurative language is saying.

8. Discuss as a class how the use of figurative language helps the reader more deeply understand the text.

Reading for First Impressions 1 (Younger Students)

1. Distribute copies of the text to students.

2. Use a projector or document camera to display the text. Demonstrate how to number each sentence in the text by putting a small number above the first word of each sentence. Have students number their sentences. Explain that they should refer to these numbers when quoting from the text.

3. Before reading, remind the class that the first read is to help them gather their initial impressions of the text. Remind them to note the following on the text using the suggested marks:

    - questions about the text (?) (write question in the margin)

    - important words, phrases, or ideas (*)

    - areas of interest or confusion (!)

    - words or phrases they want to learn more about (put box around)

    - areas of agreement or disagreement (△ = agree ▽ = disagree)

Note: You may choose to omit some text annotation options depending on the type of text being read.

4. Place students with partners and have pairs read the text aloud together. Alternative Reading Options: Read the text chorally as a class, read the text aloud to the students, or have students read the text together in small groups.

5. Ask students to share their initial impressions and questions about the text. Using the projected version of the text, model how to record ideas and questions on the text.

Reading for First Impressions 2 (Younger Students)

1. Use a projector or document camera to display the text.

2. Ask students to imagine that a classroom puppet or stuffed animal is the author of the text. Explain that the animal is going to read the text aloud.

3. Read the text aloud using a different voice to represent the puppet talking. Use your finger or a pointer to track the text.

4. Ask students to share their initial impressions of the text with the puppet. Respond to their comments using the puppet's voice. Ask, "Can you think of questions you would like to ask _____ (name of puppet or stuffed animal) about the text?" Encourage students to ask the puppet questions about unfamiliar words and confusing ideas. Have the puppet or stuffed animal answer the questions. Discuss the text as a class.

Reading for First Impressions 3 (Older Students)

1. Distribute copies of the text to students.

2. Have students number each paragraph in the passage in the left margin. Explain that they should refer to these numbers when quoting from the text. (Depending on the text, you may choose to have students number each line instead of each paragraph.)

3. Before reading, remind students that the first read is to help them gather their initial impressions of the text. Remind them to note the following on the text using the suggested marks:

   - questions about the text (?) (write question in the margin)
   - important words, phrases, or ideas (*)
   - areas of interest or confusion (!)
   - words or phrases they want to learn more about (put box around)
   - related ideas or concepts (⟨⟨⟩⟩) (write connection in the margin)
   - connections between sentences and paragraphs (←→) (draw arrows connecting)
   - areas of agreement or disagreement (△ = agree ▽ = disagree)
   - questions about credibility or sources (circle)
   - historical connections or questions (draw cloud around)
   - observations about the characters, plot, setting, etc. (underline)

Note: You may choose to omit some text annotation options depending on the type of text being read.

4. Have students read the text independently. Alternative Reading Option: Have students read the text in pairs.

5. After the initial reading is complete, provide time for students to revisit their notes and make additional annotations on the text.

6. Use a projector or document camera to display the text. Invite students to discuss their questions, thoughts, and areas of confusion. Demonstrate how to record these ideas on the text.

Reading for Inferences

1. Remind students that an inference is a conclusion that readers make by putting together evidence from the text with their own ideas and background knowledge. Give the following example: "If I tell you that there is a storm outside and the cat is hiding under the bed, what inference can you make?" Discuss how it is reasonable to infer that the cat is scared.

2. Tell students that they will use clues from the text plus their own ideas to make inferences. Explain that these inferences will help them understand the text on a deeper level.

3. Display the text using a projector or document camera. Reread the text aloud to students and have them follow along. Alternative Reading Options: Have students reread the text in pairs or independently.

4. Call students' attention to a specific area of the text. Ask, "What inferences can you make from this paragraph (section/sentence)?"

5. Draw a T-chart on the board. Label one column Text Says... and the other column I Know.... Have students differentiate between the details stated explicitly in the text and the background knowledge that they used to infer.

6. Add other examples from the text to the chart as a class.

Reading for Key Details

1. Tell students that they will be doing a close read to examine the key details in the text.

2. Place students in pairs to reread the text. Give students enough time to read the text (or just one paragraph for older students with longer texts).

3. Ask, "What did we learn in this paragraph? Sometimes, after we read a poem or story, we are still wondering about it. We have some questions that the author did not answer. For example, I wonder if _____." Remind students to refer to the text for evidence and support for their answers.

4. Record students' responses in the right-hand margin of the text so that they can view them on the projector or document camera. Instruct students to also take notes on their own copies.

5. Have students discuss the purpose of each section of text in terms of the key details provided to support the main idea as well as record any questions they may have. (You may choose to have younger students dictate their questions.)

6. If time permits, allow several students to come to the front of the class to share their questions with the class.

Reading for Main Idea

1. Display the text using a projector or document camera. Have students reread the text.

2. Ask students to identify the main points in each paragraph (or section of the text).

3. Have students discuss the main points in pairs and create a summary.

4. Invite students to share their summaries and record their ideas.

Reading for Point of View

1. Review the concept of point of view. Ask, "Who is telling the story in the text?" Help the class identify the point of view in the text passage.

2. Display the text using a projector or document camera. Select a student volunteer to reread the text aloud to the class. After listening to the text, have students turn to a partner and summarize the text using their own words.

3. Ask, "Who is telling this story? How do you know?" Allow students time to share their thoughts.

4. Think aloud as you reread the text and make notes about the narrator's point of view, highlighting specific phrases and sentences that convey this point of view.

5. As a class, discuss what the text explains and determine the point of view together.

Reading for Reasoning

1. Explain to the class that a well-written opinion piece always gives reasons that support the author's opinion.

2. Display the text using a projector or document camera. Review the author's opinion. At the top of a sheet of chart paper, write the main opinion statement from the text. Read the portion of the text that supports that opinion and ask students to identify the first reason that explains the author's opinion. Add the evidence to the chart paper.

3. Have students continue reading the text independently. Alternative Reading Options: Have students read the text in pairs or read the text aloud to them.

4. Ask students to identify the next reason that supports the author's opinion and add that to the chart paper.

5. Repeat Step 4 until all of the reasons have been identified and recorded.

Reading for Setting

1. Display the text using a projector or document camera.

2. Tell students that they will examine the development of the setting in the text.

3. Read the first paragraph (or section) aloud. Think aloud as you highlight details about the setting.

4. Have students read the rest of the text independently and highlight additional details about the setting. Alternative Reading Options: Have students read the text in pairs or small groups.

5. Allow students time to share with the class the details of the setting that they found and how the setting effected the development of the story, characters, etc.

Reading to Summarize

1. Display the text using a projector or document camera. Read the first paragraph (section) aloud.

2. Ask, "What is the central idea of this paragraph (section)?" Have students refer to specific words and sentences in the text to provide support for their responses. On the projected text, highlight the specific information that summarizes the paragraph or section.

3. Place students with partners. Provide time for pairs to reread the text and highlight the text that relates to the central idea.

4. Allow students time to record a summary of the text.

5. Invite students to share their summaries with the class.

6. As a class, create a summary of the complete text using ideas that were shared.

Reading for Text Structure 1

1. Tell students that the structure of a text is much like the structure of a house. The structure of a house is the framing and rafters that hold it together. You cannot see the structure beneath the finished product, but it is there inside the walls and ceiling.

2. Explain that the structure of a text refers to the way the ideas in the text are put together. It takes some digging to see the structure, but it is holding the text together.

3. Explain that structure is key to the effectiveness of the text. Tell students that they will examine the structure of the text to see how it helps convey the author's message or specific information.

4. Display a copy of the text using a projector or document camera. Read the first paragraph (section) aloud. Ask, "Why did the author write this paragraph?" Help students see why the author wrote the paragraph or section.

 #51505—Connect to Text: Strategies for Close Reading and Writing

5. Demonstrate how to annotate the text. Note the significance of the text structure in that paragraph or section.

6. Repeat Step 5 with the remaining paragraphs or sections.

7. Review the purpose of each paragraph or section with the class and discuss how they are connected. Analyze how each paragraph contributes to the overall text structure.

Reading for Text Structure 2

1. Using a projector or document camera, display the text.

2. Tell students that they will examine the structure of the text. Ask, "What can you tell about the text structure from a quick glance at this page?" Discuss any of the text features or visual clues about text structure.

3. Write the names of the following text structures on a sheet of chart paper: description, compare/contrast, sequence/order, cause/effect, and problem/solution. Briefly define and discuss these general text structures. (See textstructure.pdf on the Digital Resource CD.) Ask students which of these text structures best describes the text.

4. Have students reread the text independently. Alternative Reading Options: Have students read the text chorally as a class or in pairs.

5. Have students discuss in pairs which text structure they think the text follows, as well as their reasoning. Allow students to share their ideas with the class.

6. After allowing students time to respond, explain that it has a _____ text structure because it _____.

7. Provide additional time for students to share their thoughts about the relationship between the structure of the text and the author's purpose.

Reading for Text Structure 3

1. Explain to students that there are different types of texts and provide them with a visual example of a poem, an informational text, and a narrative text. Discuss characteristics of each text type.

2. Display the text for the lesson using a projector or document camera. Ask students what they notice about how the text looks (it includes short phrases on single lines, pictures with captions, illustrations, etc.).

3. Have students reread the text in pairs. Ask, "What type of text do you think this is? How can you tell?" Alternative Reading Options: Have students read the text chorally or read it aloud to them.

4. Confirm the text type with students and point out its distinguishing characteristics.

Reading for Theme

1. Display the text using a projector or document camera. Have students reread the text independently.

2. Tell students that they must write a summary of the text in their own words, and it must include the text's main idea and key details.

3. Place students in small groups. After students have written their summaries, ask one representative from each group to read the summary aloud. Record the summaries or display them using a projector or document camera.

4. Explain to students the concept of theme/central message.

5. Ask students to analyze the summaries for key similarities/messages and have them use this information to decide on the theme(s) of the text as a class.

Reading for Word Choice

1. Display the text using a projector or document camera. Read the text aloud while students listen and follow along. Alternative Reading Options: Have students read independently or in pairs.

2. Ask students to circle important words that the author uses more than once.

3. Discuss these repeated words with the class. Ask, "Why do you think the author chose to repeat these words? What effect does the repetition of these words have on the text?" Remind students to support their answers with evidence from the text.

Reading for Word Meaning 1

1. Display the text using a projector or document camera. Have students reread the text independently or in pairs.

2. Select key words from the text that need to be defined and display those words for students.

3. Ask students to highlight the sentences where those words are found and that give their definitions.

4. Ask, "Why do you think the author put the words _____ and _____ in italics (or bold)?" Discuss how the text features help the reader determine the meanings of these words and phrases.

Reading for Word Meaning 2

1. Display the text using a projector or document camera. Have students review their initial impression notes in the margins. Ask if anyone noted any words that were either confusing or interesting in the text. Highlight these words on the projected text.

 #51505—Connect to Text: Strategies for Close Reading and Writing

2. Have students reread the text independently or in pairs.

3. Allow students time to use dictionaries, context clues, and other resources to determine the meanings of unknown or confusing words and phrases.

4. Have students share their definitions and then agree on a definition for each word as a class. Record the definition on the displayed text and have students do the same.

Reading for Visual Media

1. Ask, "Why do some informational texts include charts, graphs, maps, and other graphics?" Explain that these visuals provide additional details.

2. Display the text using a projector or document camera. Direct students' attention to a specific piece of visual media in the text. Make sure students understand how to read it appropriately.

3. Ask students to examine a different picture or image from the text and read the caption(s). Discuss their observations.

4. Ask, "How do these visuals help readers understand the text better?" Remind students to use evidence from the text to support their answers.

5. Ask, "How else could the author have presented this information? Why do you think the author chose this format?" Discuss how the visual presentation complements the text.

Writing from Informational Texts

1. Review the aspects of informational text covered in the close reading activities (e.g., key details, word meaning, and visual media).

2. Tell students that they will be using what they learned to write their own informational texts.

3. Have students select a topic for their writing and refer back to the close reading text as a mentor text for structure and style.

4. Allow students time to write and revise.

5. Invite students to share their completed work in pairs, small groups, or with the entire class.

Writing from Opinion/Argument Text

1. Ask students a question based on the topic of the close reading text. Have students discuss their opinions in small groups.

2. Tell students that no matter what they personally believe, they will write an opinion piece in support of the issue.

3. As a class, brainstorm opinions and reasons that support the issue. List these on chart paper.

4. List transition words and phrases (i.e., for instance, for example, in addition to, furthermore, additionally) on a sheet of chart paper. Explain that these words and phrases help readers connect the ideas in texts.

5. Allow students time to outline their writing. Remind them to use at least three linking words or phrases from the class chart.

6. After writing is complete, have each student read his or her opinion aloud to a partner. Encourage students to give their partners two compliments and one suggestion for improvement.

Writing from Narrative Text 1

1. Review the aspects of narrative text covered in the close reading activities (e.g., main idea, characters, and point of view).

2. Tell students that they will have a chance to write their own story that is similar in approach to the text for close reading (e.g., personal narrative or poem).

3. Conduct a whole-class brainstorming session. Record students' ideas on chart paper.

4. Provide time for students to plan their story. Demonstrate how to elaborate on the basic outline based on the type of text the students are writing.

5. Provide students time to write their stories.

6. If possible, display the finished stories on a classroom or hallway bulletin board or bind them into a class book.

Writing from Narrative Text 2

1. Review the aspects of narrative text covered in the close reading activities (e.g., main idea, characters, and point of view).

2. Display a portion of the close reading text using a projector or document camera. Discuss how the text would differ if it were written from a different point of view (e.g., first person or third person).

3. Tell students that they are going to rewrite the text (or a portion of the text) using the _____ person point of view. Explain that this is not just an exercise in replacing pronouns. Instead, students must think about adding dialogue and using figurative language to support the change in perspective.

4. Provide time for students to complete the writing activity independently.

5. Place students with partners and have them read their work aloud to each other. Make sure students give one general compliment and one suggestion to improve their partner's work.

6. Allow students time to make revisions to their work.

7. Invite volunteers to read their work aloud to the class. Discuss how point of view affects the way authors express feelings and events in their writing.

8. If possible, display the finished stories on a bulletin board.

Connect to Informational Text

Informational text plays an important role in both reading and writing instruction. In the past, the majority of reading and writing activities, especially in the elementary grades, focused on narrative literature. Under the Common Core and other state standards, however, there has been a dramatic shift to include increasing amounts of informational text. In kindergarten, there is a 50/50 split between informational and literary text, and this balance gradually shifts to a 70/30 split by high school (NGA and CCSSO 2010a).

What Is Informational Text?

It is clear that schools and educators need to include more informational texts in the classroom, but the definition of "informational text" is not always clear. The Common Core uses a broad definition of informational texts that includes both traditional nonfiction texts, such as texts that contain factual information about science, social studies, and history, as well as literary nonfiction and technical texts (NGA and CCSSO 2010a). According to Maloch and Bomer (2013), the term *literary nonfiction text* generally refers to "a range of genres that attempt to represent the real world while also employing characteristics of literature" (209). Examples of these types of texts include biographies, autobiographies, and memoirs. Technical texts include documents such as instruction manuals, signs, directions, brochures, advertisements, and information displayed in graphs, charts, maps, and other visual formats. Texts that present claims, arguments, and opinions are also typically categorized as informational text. (See pages 81–84 for more information on argument texts.)

Informational Text and Today's Standards

The Common Core outlines the skills and knowledge that students must demonstrate when reading factual and technical texts. These include critical thinking, reasoning, and evidence collection skills. The three categories include key ideas and details, craft and structure, and integration of knowledge and ideas. Within each of these categories, there are three standards that describe specific reading comprehension skills. Close reading activities help students connect to informational texts and allow them to practice the skills in all three categories.

Close Reading and Informational Text

Key Ideas and Details

When addressing key ideas and details, close reading activities for informational text focus on three main skills:

1. **Citing evidence to support both explicit and inferred concepts from the text.** Close reading provides an excellent tool for helping students notice the difference between what the text says explicitly and what can be inferred from the text. Through the process of exploring a small segment of text, students learn how to cite evidence directly from the text to support information learned explicitly as well as inferences made from the text.

2. **Identifying and analyzing the development of the main idea and the key supporting details in the text.** Close reading helps students isolate the important concepts in a text and examine the ways in which the author builds these concepts through word choice, text structure, and point of view.

3. **Recognizing and explaining connections among individuals, events, and ideas within the text.** Often, students are able to identify these central elements in a text, but they have little understanding of how or why these elements interact. Through close reading, students learn how to examine the relationships among these elements and recognize how they work together to convey meaning.

Craft and Structure

Craft and structure focus on the ways in which word choice, text structure, and point of view or purpose affect the overall text. The structure of informational text is generally quite distinct from the narrative text structure (literary nonfiction being an exception), and close reading allows students to examine the structure of a text at the level of the word, sentence, and paragraph. The ability to recognize and use the distinctive text features of informational text enables students to extract information and meaning from a text more effectively. Furthermore, close reading can be used to help students identify the author's point of view or purpose. By directing attention to specific aspects of the text, students learn to see how the author's point of view or purpose helps shape the overall structure and content of the text.

Integration of Knowledge and Ideas

Integration of knowledge and ideas requires students to expand their analysis of informational text to include concepts presented in a variety of formats (visually, electronically, etc.) and across multiple texts. This type of analysis can be quite daunting initially, but close reading activities help students break down the task into manageable segments. Informational texts often include graphics, such as maps, diagrams, graphs, charts, etc., and students do not always pay adequate attention to these text features. Close reading directs the students' attention to these important elements and helps them become accustomed to including them in text analysis. Furthermore, close reading is instrumental in teaching students how to compare and contrast multiple texts. By isolating important aspects of multiple texts, close reading shows students how to identify the similarities and differences in the structure and presentation of information between two or more texts.

Writing Informational Text

Three main types of writing are opinion/argument, informative/explanatory, and narrative. For informative/explanatory writing, students are required to "examine and convey complex ideas, concepts, and information clearly and accurately through the effective selection, organization, and analysis of content" (NGA and CCSSO 2010a).

Close reading an informational text gives students a deeper understanding of both the content and the structure of the text. As a result, close reading of informational texts can improve students' writing in two ways. First, informational texts can be used as sources for explanatory writing. Students must support their answers, ideas, and claims with information drawn directly from the text. This means teaching students to include specific facts, details, quotations, and ideas from the text as evidence and support for the content of their writing (also known as writing from a source). By using close reading activities to analyze a text, students learn how to extract the relevant information needed to provide support for their textual analyses.

In addition to using close reading to explore informational texts as a source for writing, close reading can also turn reading assignments into mentor texts. Mentor texts are texts students use to learn about different writing styles, techniques, and structures that they can transfer to their own writing. For example, a teacher might design a close reading activity to help students study how an informational text uses a problem/solution text structure to explain a scientific discovery. Following the close reading activity, the teacher then asks the students to apply their new understanding of the problem/solution text structure to their own explanatory writing. In this example, the students use the informational text as a mentor text to learn about, and then apply, the problem/solution text structure. Regardless of the specific writing activity, close reading enables students to access informational text on a deeper level and provides them with tools to improve their writing skills.

Text-Dependent Questions and Prompts to Support Close Reading and Writing of Informational Text

The following text-dependent questions and prompts cover some of the broad areas of focus in literacy. When planning close reading and writing activities, these questions and prompts should be tailored to fit the selected text passages and age/readiness level of your students.

Key Ideas and Details

- What information is stated explicitly in the text selection? What can you infer from the passage? Cite evidence from the text to support your answer.

- What is the central idea of the text? How does the author develop this idea over the course of the text?

- List some of the key details from the text. How do these details support the central idea of the text? Refer to the text for specific information about these details.

- Provide an objective summary of the text. Be sure not to include your personal opinions or judgments in your summary.

- What or who are the important individuals/events/ideas in the text? How does the author develop these elements? How do these elements interact over the course of the text?

Craft and Structure

- How does the author's choice of words affect the overall meaning or tone of the text?

- How do the text features help the reader comprehend the text?

- What type of structure does the author use in the text? How do you know?

- How does the author divide the text? How are the parts of the text related?

- What is the author's point of view in the text? How was this point of view conveyed?

- What is the purpose of the text? How do you know? Refer to the text for specific examples to support your answer.

Integration of Knowledge and Ideas

- How do the visual elements in the text contribute to its overall meaning?
- How does the format of the text (visual, auditory, digital, etc.) effect the reader's understanding of the information?
- How are the two (or more) texts the same? How are they different?
- How do the multiple texts address similar themes or concepts?

I Can Work

Overview

The close reading of this passage focuses on teaching the students how information is connected within a piece of text. Although this text sample is very short, the components of the text interact in several ways. First, students examine how the sentences of written text are connected. Each sentence builds on the sentence before it to provide the reader with more information and detail about the topic. Then, students identify the two individuals in the text, the narrator and his mother, and consider how their relationship impacts the text. While it is common for parents to help their children, in this text, the boy helps his mother and, as a result, feels proud. Finally, the last close reading activity helps students identify the relationship between the written text and the graphics. By examining the photograph that accompanies the text, students learn how visual elements often add details that are not provided in the text. Together, these close reading activities illustrate how several text components work together to convey information and meaning in a variety of ways. At the end of the lesson, students apply their new learning to create their own informational text based on the format and structure of the sample text.

Standards

- With prompting and support, ask and answer questions about key details in a text.
- With prompting and support, describe the connection between two individuals, events, ideas, or pieces of information in a text.
- With prompting and support, describe the relationship between illustrations and the text in which they appear.
- Use a combination of drawing, dictating, and writing to compose informative/explanatory texts in which they name what they are writing about and supply some information about the topic.

Areas of Focus

- key details
- connecting information
- visual media
- connecting drawing and writing

Materials

- *I Can Work* (page 39)
- *Feeling Proud* (page 42)
- *Helping Hand* (page 43)
- *Kids Can Work* (pages 44–45)
- projector or document camera
- chart paper
- coloring supplies

I Can Work

I can work. I help Mom. I feel proud!

Close Reading Activities

First Read (Overview/First Impressions)

1. Distribute copies of the *I Can Work* text (page 39) to students.

2. Use a projector or document camera to display the text. Demonstrate how to number each sentence in the text by putting a small number above the first word of each sentence. Have students number their sentences. Explain that they should refer to these numbers when quoting from the text.

3. Before reading, remind the class that the first read is to help them gather their initial impressions of the text. Remind them to note the following on the text using the suggested marks:

   - questions about the text (?) (write question in the margin)
   - important words or ideas (*)
   - areas of interest or confusion (!)

4. Place students with partners and have pairs read the text aloud together.

5. Ask students to share their initial impressions and questions about the text. Using the projected version of the text, model how to record ideas and questions on the text.

Second Read (Key Details)

1. Copy the sentences from the text onto a sheet of chart paper. Leave space between each sentence.

2. Read the first sentence aloud to the class. Ask students, "What does the author mean by 'work'? How do you know?"

3. Discuss how the second sentence relates to the first sentence. Explain that the second sentence clarifies the first sentence by giving an example. In this case, the boy's "work" is helping his mom.

4. Discuss how the third sentence relates to the other sentences. Explain that the third sentence gives even more details by telling how the boy feels about the work.

5. Distribute copies of the *Feeling Proud* activity sheet (page 42) to students. Read the instructions aloud to the class. Have students read the focus question aloud together. Remind the class to include details from the text to support their answers. Provide time for students to complete the activity sheets independently.

Third Read (Connecting Information)

1. Have the students reread the text.

2. Ask them to identify the two people in the text and how they are connected (e.g., *the boy helping his mom*).

3. Ask, "Why does the boy feel proud after he helps his mom?" Discuss their answers as a class.

4. Distribute copies of the *Helping Hand* activity sheet (page 43) to students. Have them draw a picture showing how they help at home.

Fourth Read (Visual Media)

1. Tell students to examine the picture in the text. Ask, "What does the picture show?"

2. Display the chart paper with the three sentences created during the second read activity. Read the text aloud to the class.

3. Ask, "What information can we learn from the picture that is not in the written text?" Discuss how the picture shows that the boy helps his mom by doing the dishes, a detail that is not included in the written text.

Writing Connection

Preparation Note

Duplicate pages 44–45 and cut each page in half on the dotted line. Assemble the books by stapling the four half-sheets together on the left side of the paper. Make enough books for each student to have one.

1. Review the aspects of informational text covered in the close reading activities (key details, connected information, and visual media). Tell students that they will be using what they learned to make their own informational texts.

2. Distribute copies of the *Kids Can Work* book to students. Read each page of the book together. Show students how to fill in the blank lines with words to complete the sentences. Model how to illustrate each page.

3. Provide time for students to complete their *Kids Can Work* books independently.

4. When the students have completed their books, have them find a partner and take turns reading their books aloud.

Feeling Proud

Directions: Draw a picture and write a sentence to answer the question below.

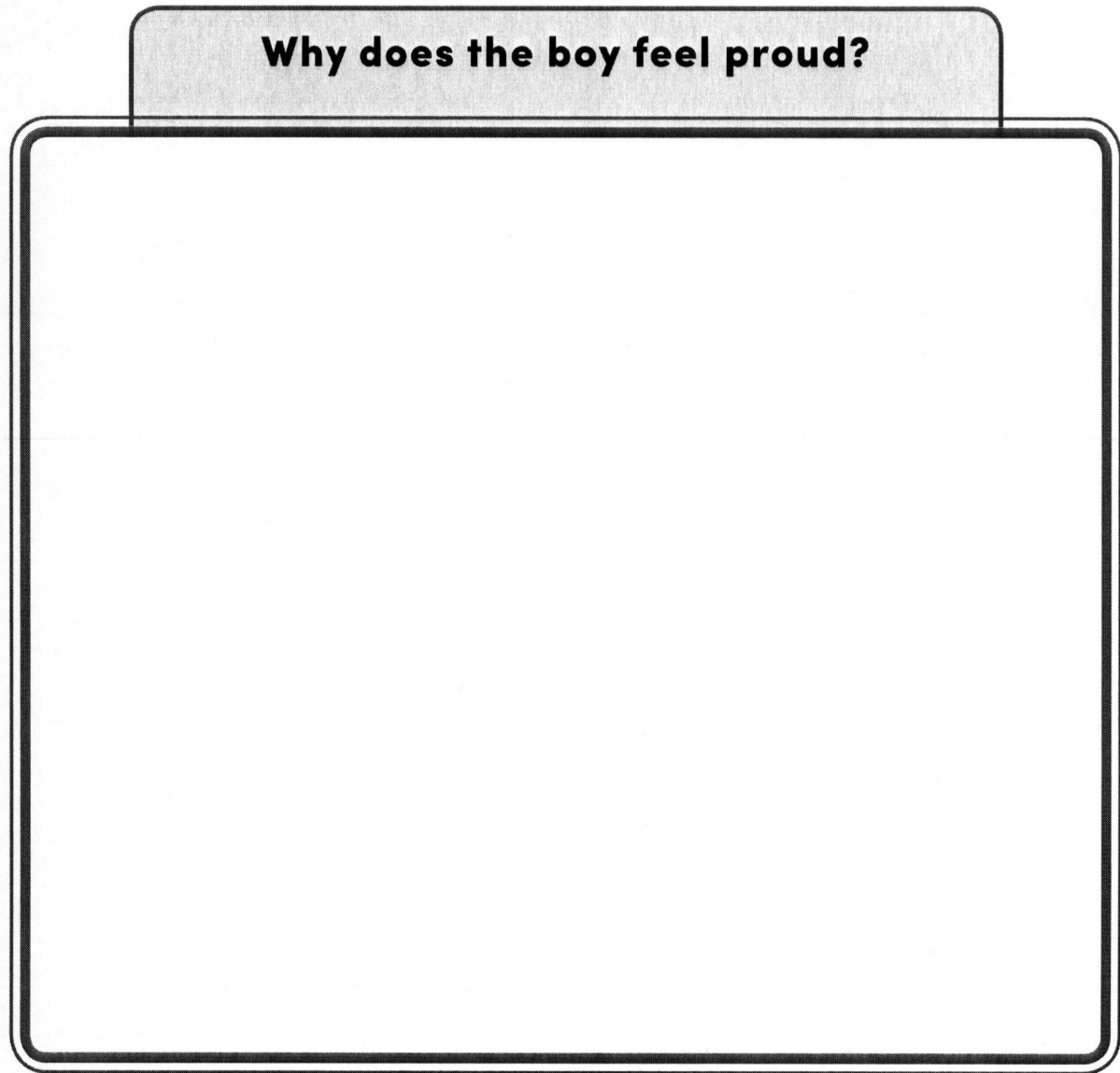

Why does the boy feel proud?

The boy feels proud. He can _____

_____

_____ .

 #51505—Connect to Text: Strategies for Close Reading and Writing

Name: _____ **Date:** _____

Helping Hand

Directions: Draw a picture to show how you help your family at home. Label your drawing.

Name: _____ **Date:** _____

Kids Can Work

By: _____

Kids can _____ .

Name: _____ **Date:** _____

Kids can _____ .

They feel _____ !

Choices

Overview

The close reading of this text focuses on determining the main idea, using context to determine word meaning, and analyzing how graphics contribute to the reader's understanding of a text. First, students identify the central idea of the text, which is explicitly stated in the third sentence. Next, students identify and circle important and repeated words in the text and analyze the impact of word choice on meaning. They dig even deeper into the text to analyze how the author employs examples to clarify the meaning of a key word. Finally, students examine visual elements to learn how pictures can help them better understand a text.

Standards

- Determine the main idea of a text; recount the key details and explain how they support the main idea.
- Determine the meaning of general academic and domain-specific words and phrases in a text relevant to a grade appropriate topic or subject area.
- Use information gained from illustrations and the words in a text to demonstrate understanding of the text.
- Introduce a topic and group related information together; include illustrations when useful to aiding comprehension.

Areas of Focus

- main idea
- word meaning
- visual media
- illustrations as visual aids

Materials

- *Choices* (page 47)
- *Saving and Spending* (page 50)
- *Picture Detectives* (page 51)
- *Money Choices* (page 52)
- projector or document camera
- highlighters
- coloring supplies

Choices

When you buy things, you give up your money. You trade your money for something else.

Buying things is a choice, but sometimes it is a necessary choice. It is smart to buy the things you need.

Sometimes buying things is not necessary. You may buy things you want, but do not need. When you do this, you make a choice.

A doll is something you want.

Food is something you need.

Close Reading Activities

First Read (Overview/First Impressions)

1. Distribute copies of the *Choices* text (page 47) to students.

2. Use a projector or document camera to display the text. Demonstrate how to number each line of the passage on the left side of the text. Have students number their copies. Explain that they should refer to these numbers when quoting from the text.

3. Before reading the passage, remind students that the first read is to help them gather their initial impressions of the text. Ask them to note any of the following topics directly on the text during the reading using the suggested marks:

    - questions about the text (?) (write question in the margin)

    - words or phrases they want to learn more about (put box around)

    - words or phrases that seem important (*)

    - areas of interest or confusion (!)

4. Read the text chorally as a class.

5. Provide time for students to revisit their notes and make additional annotations.

6. Use a projector or document camera to display the text. Have students share their questions, thoughts, and areas of confusion. Demonstrate how to record these on the text.

Second Read (Main Idea)

1. Read the text aloud while students listen and follow along.

2. Have students reread the text independently. Ask them to circle important words that the author uses more than once (e.g., *choice, necessary, need*).

3. Discuss these repeated words with the class. Ask, "Why do you think the author chose to repeat these words? What effect does the repetition of these words have on the text?" Remind students to support their answers with evidence from the text.

4. Have students work in pairs to complete the questions on the *Saving and Spending* activity sheet (page 50). Remind them to use evidence from the text to support their statements.

Third Read (Word Meaning)

1. Have students reread the text. This time, ask them to underline the word *choice*.

2. Remind students that there are several ways to determine the meaning of an unknown word. You can use an external resource, like a dictionary, to find the definition. You can also use context clues within the text.

3. Have students search the text for details that could help readers determine the meaning of the word *choice*. Ask them to highlight the helpful phrases and sentences.

4. Point out that the sentence, "You may buy things you want, but do not need," is an example of *choice*. Explain that examples help us to better understand words in context.

Fourth Read (Visual Media)

1. Ask students to examine the two pictures and read the captions. Discuss their observations.

2. Ask, "How do these images help readers understand the text better?" Remind students to use evidence from the text to support their answers.

3. Distribute copies of the *Picture Detectives* activity sheet (page 51). Have students complete the activity sheet independently. Remind them to use evidence from the text to support their answers.

Writing Connection

1. Review the aspects of informational text covered in the close reading activities (central idea, word meaning, and visual media).

2. Distribute copies of the *Money Choices* activity sheet (page 52) to students.

3. Read the directions aloud. Remind students to refer back to the text for evidence, examples, and specific words and phrases to support their ideas. Highlight the box on the activity sheet and explain that their illustration should support the ideas presented in their writing.

4. Have students work independently to complete the writing activity on the *Money Choices* activity sheet.

5. If time permits, allow students to share their writing with partners. Display the students' paragraphs and illustrations on a classroom bulletin board.

Saving and Spending

Directions: Read the text. Answer the questions below in your own words.

1. What is the main idea of the text? How do you know?

_____

_____

_____

_____

_____

2. What are two key details that tell you more about the main idea?

_____

_____

_____

_____

_____

Picture Detectives

Directions: Read the text. Look at the pictures. Answer the questions below.

1. How does the first picture tell you more about the main idea of the text?

_____

_____

_____

_____

_____

2. How does the second picture tell you more about the main idea of the text?

_____

_____

_____

_____

_____

Name: _____ **Date:** _____

Money Choices

Directions: Write a paragraph to answer the questions below. Refer to the text for evidence to support your answers.

> What is the main idea of the text passage? What text features communicate this idea to the reader?

_____

_____

_____

_____

_____

Directions: Draw an illustration that also answers the questions. Like in the text you read, your illustration should provide more information to readers.

Ordering Whole Numbers

Overview

As students progress in school, they are expected to learn new information by reading informational texts. Reading to learn requires students to successfully decode text, extract key ideas, understand vocabulary, and connect new information to their schema. In this lesson, students apply several close reading strategies to a math text. They practice using text features and definitions of key words to connect concepts within the text. They also analyze the relationship between text structure and the purpose of the text and then apply information from multiple texts to solve a problem. In the writing connection, students reflect on the skills they learned in the close reading activities by describing the steps they took to complete the math task based on the text.

Areas of Focus

- word meaning
- text structure
- applying and analyzing sources
- using precise language and vocabulary

Materials

- *Ordering Whole Numbers* (page 54)
- *Ascending and Descending Order* (page 58)
- *Text Structure and Author's Purpose* (page 59)
- *Ranking Wealth* (page 60)
- *Task Analysis* (page 61)
- projector or document camera
- highlighters
- chart paper

Standards

- Explain the relationships or interactions between two or more individuals, events, ideas, or concepts in a historical, scientific, or technical text based on specific information in the text.
- Determine the meaning of general academic and domain-specific words and phrases in a text relevant to a grade appropriate topic or subject area.
- Compare and contrast the overall structure of events, ideas, concepts, or information in two or more texts.
- Draw on information from multiple print or digital sources, demonstrating the ability to locate an answer to a question quickly or to solve a problem efficiently.
- Use precise language and domain-specific vocabulary to inform about or explain the topic.

Ordering Whole Numbers

To *ascend* means to go up. Putting numbers in **ascending order** means to list them from least to greatest. The numbers 1, 7, 12, 14, and 37 are listed in ascending order.

To *descend* means to go down. Putting numbers in **descending order** means to list them from greatest to least. The numbers 103, 75, 52, 14, and 7 are listed in descending order.

How to Order Numbers

Step 1: Line the numbers up by place values.	1,653,000,000 1,637,000,000
Step 2: Beginning with the greatest place (the one farthest left), compare the digits.	**1**,653,000,000 **1**,637,000,000
Step 3: If those digits are equal, continue to the right. Compare each place value until you find a difference. If you do not find a difference, the two numbers are equal.	1,6**5**3,000,000 1,6**3**7,000,000
Step 4: Write the numbers in whichever order is called for.	**Ascending order:** 1,637,000,000 1,653,000,000 **Descending order:** 1,653,000,000 1,637,000,000

#51505—*Connect to Text: Strategies for Close Reading and Writing*   © Shell Education

Close Reading Activities

First Read (Overview/First Impressions)

1. Distribute copies of the *Ordering Whole Numbers* text (page 54) to students.

2. Use a projector or document camera to display the text. Demonstrate how to number each line of the passage on the left side of the text. Have students number their copies. Explain that they should refer to these numbers when quoting from the text.

3. Before reading, remind students that the first read is to help them gather their initial impressions of the text. Remind them to note the following on the text using the suggested marks:

    • questions about the text (?) (write question in the margin)

    • words or phrases they want to learn more about (put box around)

    • words or phrases that seem important (*)

    • areas of interest or confusion (!)

4. Place students in pairs to partner-read the text. Students can choose how they want to take turns.

5. After the initial reading is complete, provide time for students to revisit their notes and make additional annotations on the text.

6. Use a projector or document camera to display the text. Invite students to discuss their questions, thoughts, and areas of confusion. Demonstrate how to record these ideas on the text.

Second Read (Word Meaning)

1. Have students reread the text independently.

2. Ask students to highlight the sentences that give definitions of the words *ascend* and *descend*.

3. Ask, "Why do you think the author put the words *ascend* and *descend* in italics and the terms *ascending order* and *descending order* in bold?" Discuss how these text features help the reader determine the meanings of these words and phrases.

4. Distribute copies of the *Ascending and Descending Order* activity sheet (page 58) to students. Read the question aloud.

5. Give students 2–3 minutes to discuss the question with a partner.

6. Have students complete the *Ascending and Descending Order* activity sheet independently. Remind them to go back to the text to find supporting evidence for their answers.

7. Provide time for students to share their responses with the class. Discuss the importance of text features in informational texts.

Third Read (Text Structure)

1. Using a projector or document camera, demonstrate how to draw a horizontal line between the top portion of the written text and the chart containing the step-by-step instructions below it. Have students draw the same line on their copies.

2. Tell students that they will examine the structure of these two sections of text. Ask, "What can you tell about the text structure from a quick glance at this page?" Discuss how some of the text is presented in a chart format while some is presented in paragraph format.

3. Have students reread the top portion of text. Ask, "What was the author's purpose for writing these paragraphs?" (*to define the concepts of ascending and descending order of numbers*) Remind students to cite text evidence for their ideas during the discussion.

4. Write the names of the following text structures on a sheet of chart paper: *description, compare/contrast, sequence/order, cause/effect,* and *problem/ solution.* Briefly define and discuss these general text structures. (See textstructure.pdf on the Digital Resource CD.) Ask students which of these text structures best describes the top portion of the text.

5. After allowing students to respond, explain that it has a "description" text structure because it describes ascending and descending order and provides examples.

6. Direct students' attention to the bottom portion of the text. Have them make observations about the structure of this portion. (*numbered steps, chart format, etc.*) Ask, "What was the author's purpose for writing this section of text?" Discuss how the text structure supports the author's purpose.

7. Distribute copies of the *Text Structure and Author's Purpose* activity sheet (page 59) to students. Read the directions aloud. Have students complete the activity sheet independently or with partners.

8. Provide time for students to share their responses and discuss the relationship between the structure of a text and the author's purpose.

Fourth Read (Applying and Analyzing Sources)

1. Distribute a copy of the *Ranking Wealth* activity sheet (page 60) to each student. Have students read the text at the top of the page independently.

2. Read the text aloud and answer students' questions about the activity sheet. Tell students that they will need to use information from the *Ordering Whole Numbers* text (page 54) and the *Ranking Wealth* text to complete the task.

3. Place students in pairs. Give each pair a highlighter or yellow marker. Ask them to highlight the information on both texts that is necessary for completing the *Ranking Wealth* task.

4. Provide time for the students to complete the task on the *Ranking Wealth* activity sheet.

Writing Connection

1. Review the aspects of informational text covered in the close reading activities. (*word meaning, connecting concepts, text structure, and applying information from multiple sources*)

2. Tell students that they will use the information and skills they learned to explain how they completed the task on the *Ranking Wealth* activity sheet.

3. Display the *Task Analysis* activity sheet (page 61) using a projector or document camera. Model for students how to explain their work on the task by writing Step 1 together as a class. For example, you might write, "First, I learned the definitions of the terms *ascending order* and *descending order* from the *Ordering Whole Numbers* text."

4. Tell students that their written descriptions should include at least five steps. For English language learners and below-level learners, make a T-chart on the board. Label the left column, *How I did it*. Label the right column, *Why I did it*. Have students explain their work step-by-step as you record their ideas on the T-chart.

5. Encourage students to refer back to the text as often as possible in their descriptions of their problem-solving processes. Remind them to use precise and appropriate vocabulary words from the text in their written descriptions.

6. Provide time for students to complete the *Task Analysis* activity sheet independently.

7. Provide time for students to read their explanations aloud with partners.

Name: _____ **Date:** _____

Ascending and Descending Order

Directions: After reading the text, answer the question below.

Using your own words, describe how the concepts of ascending order and descending order are related. Remember to refer to the text for evidence to support your answer.

_____

_____

_____

_____

_____

_____

_____

_____

_____

_____

_____

_____

_____

_____

Name: _____ **Date:** _____

Text Structure and Author's Purpose

Directions: Choose two of the topics listed below. For each topic, explain the type of text structure you would use and why this text structure fits the purpose.

Topics	Types of Text Structures
• Items to pack on a camping trip • Soccer vs. baseball • The best type of pet • Directions to get to a friend's house • Gifts you hope to receive for your birthday	• Description • Compare/Contrast • Sequence/Order • Cause/Effect • Problem/Solution

Topic #1: _____

Type of text structure: _____

Why this text structure fits the purpose of the topic:

_____

_____

_____

Topic #2: _____

Type of text structure: _____

Why this text structure fits the purpose of the topic:

_____

_____

_____

Name: _____ **Date:** _____

Ranking Wealth

Directions: Read the text below. Refer to the *Ordering Whole Numbers* text for more information. Then, complete the task.

In 2010, the five richest people in the world were thought to be:

- Carlos Slim Helú of Mexico with $53,500,000,000
- Lakshmi Mittal of India with $28,700,000,000
- Mukesh Ambani of India with $29,000,000,000
- Warren Buffet of the United States with $47,000,000,000
- William Gates III of the United States with $53,000,000,000

Task

Put these billionaires in descending order based on their wealth.

 #51505—Connect to Text: Strategies for Close Reading and Writing

Name: _____   **Date:** _____

Task Analysis

Directions: Write a step-by-step explanation of how you completed the *Ranking Wealth* task. Refer to the two texts you used for the task. Tell specifically how each text helped you complete the steps.

1. _____

_____

_____

2. _____

_____

_____

3. _____

_____

_____

4. _____

_____

_____

5. _____

_____

_____

Hatshepsut: The Female Pharaoh

Standards

- Analyze in detail how a key individual, event, or idea is introduced, illustrated, and elaborated in a text.
- Analyze how a particular sentence, paragraph, chapter, or section fits into the overall structure of a text and contributes to the development of the ideas.
- Determine an author's point of view or purpose in a text and explain how it is conveyed in the text.
- Introduce a topic; organize ideas, concepts, and information, using strategies such as definition, classification, comparison/contrast, and cause/effect; include formatting, graphics, and multimedia when useful to aiding comprehension.

Overview

This biographical text describes the rise to power of Hatshepsut, Egypt's first female pharaoh. Biographies provide opportunities to study text structure as it is applied to the story of a person's life. In this case, students read the text closely to see how the author conveys various types of information about Hatshepsut. Next, students dig even deeper into the text to analyze the details contained within a single sentence. They then analyze how that sentence fits into the overall structure of the paragraph and the entire passage. Finally, students examine the author's word choices to determine point of view and purpose. In the writing connection activity, students apply what they have learned to write an informational text using the cause/effect text structure.

Areas of Focus

- key details
- text structure
- point of view
- organizational structure

Materials

- *Hatshepsut: The Female Pharaoh* (page 63)
- *Traits of Hatshepsut* (page 67)
- *Sentence Analysis* (page 68)
- *Hatshepsut: Patient or Power-Hungry?* (page 69)
- *Cause and Effect* (page 70)
- *The Female Pharaoh* (page 71)
- projector or document camera
- highlighters

Hatshepsut: The Female Pharaoh

Many people have called Hatshepsut (hat-**shep**-soot) the greatest woman in Egypt's history. Before her time, no woman had ever ruled Egypt. Hatshepsut's father was Thutmose I (thoot-**moh**-s*uh*). When he died, there was no son in direct line to become pharaoh, so Hatshepsut became an important part of Egypt's history.

A Royal Birth

Hatshepsut was born around 1508 bc. Her father, the pharaoh, was Thutmose I. He ruled the whole country. Thutmose I had more than one wife. The first one, the great queen, Queen Ahmose (ah-**moh**-*suh*), was Hatshepsut's mother. Hatshepsut also had two brothers and one sister, but none of them lived to be adults. She knew her father must have missed his sons, so she sometimes wore boy's clothing to make him feel better.

An Empty Throne

When Hatshepsut was a teenager, her father died. Even though Egyptian girls and women had many rights, the pharaoh had always been a male. Would the Egyptians allow a young woman to rule them? Hatshepsut was a strong young woman who wanted to lead others. She could read and write. She also liked to learn new things. She had watched her father while he ruled as pharaoh, and Hatshepsut had many ideas about how to make Egypt great.

Thutmose I did have a son, Thutmose II, but the boy was not in line to be the new pharaoh because his mother was not the pharaoh's first wife. Young Hatshepsut's advisors gave her an idea. If she married her half brother, she and Thutmose II could rule Egypt together!

The Power Behind the Throne

During this time, Thutmose II was the pharaoh. Hatshepsut was only his regent, but she was really the person who led Egypt through some of its best years. Hatshepsut was very strong willed and intelligent. In fact, she was smarter than Thutmose II. She was also in better health. She made most of the decisions about the nation, and the priests and other leaders of Egypt followed her advice.

Thutmose II ruled for about 10 years with Hatshepsut as his regent. He died young, and his son from another woman, Thutmose III, became pharaoh. Thutmose III was only a baby so Hatshepsut continued to rule as regent. As time passed, Thutmose III faded further into the background at the palace.

Hatshepsut Takes the Throne

In about 1473 bc, Hatshepsut declared herself pharaoh. She took the throne and ruled Egypt for about 22 years. She was well respected. She brought energy and wisdom to Egypt's history. When she died, Thutmose III became the new pharaoh.

Close Reading Activities

First Read (Overview/First Impressions)

1. Distribute copies of the *Hatshepsut: The Female Pharaoh* text (page 63) to students.

2. Have students number each paragraph in the passage in the left margin. Explain that they should refer to these numbers when quoting from the text.

3. Before reading, remind students that the first read is to help them gather their initial impressions of the text. Remind them to note the following on the text using the suggested marks:

   - questions about the text (?) (write question in margin)

   - words or phrases they want to learn more about (put box around)

   - words or phrases that seem important (*)

   - areas of interest or confusion (!)

   - related ideas or concepts (⬭) (write connection in the margin)

   - connections between sentences and paragraphs (◄—►) (draw arrows connecting)

4. Have students read the text independently.

5. After the initial reading is complete, provide time for students to revisit their notes and make additional annotations on the text.

6. Use a projector or document camera to display the text. Invite students to discuss their questions, thoughts, and areas of confusion. Demonstrate how to record these ideas on the text.

Second Read (Key Details)

1. Tell students that they will be doing a close read to examine how the author introduces, illustrates, and elaborates on the life of Hatshepsut over the course of the text.

2. Place students in pairs to read the text paragraph by paragraph. Give students enough time to read one paragraph. Then ask, "What did we learn about Hatshepsut in this paragraph?" Remind students to refer to the text for evidence and support for their answers. Record students' responses in the right-hand margin of the text so they can view them on the projector or document camera. Instruct students to also take notes on their own texts.

3. Have students discuss the purpose of each section of text in terms of the development and description of Hatshepsut.

4. Distribute copies of the *Traits of Hatshepsut* activity sheet (page 67) to students. Read the directions aloud.

5. Display the *Traits of Hatshepsut* activity sheet using a projector or document camera. Reread the first sentence of the text aloud to the class. Ask, "What word would you use to describe Hatshepsut based on this sentence?" Demonstrate how to complete the first row by writing the word *famous* (or a similar word suggested by the class) in the "Adjective" column. In the space labeled "Textual evidence or support," record the sentence from the text, "Many people have called Hatshepsut the greatest woman in Egypt's history."

6. Provide time for students to complete the *Traits of Hatshepsut* activity sheet with their partners.

7. Provide time for students to share their responses with the class.

Third Read (Text Structure)

1. Have students reread the section titled "A Royal Birth" independently.

2. Ask, "What do you notice about the last sentence in this paragraph?" Discuss how the last sentence provides an example of Hatshepsut's actions.

3. Distribute copies of the *Sentence Analysis* activity sheet (page 68) to students and display the activity sheet using a projector or document camera.

4. Read the phrase, "She knew her father must have missed his sons...." Ask, "What can we infer from this part of the sentence?" Discuss how that phrase tells us that her father had loved and cherished his sons.

5. Repeat Step 4 for the second part of the sentence, "...so she sometimes wore boy's clothing to make him feel better." Explain how readers can infer details about Hatshepsut's character, as well as historical Egyptian society and culture, from that phrase.

6. Divide students into small groups of 3–4 students. Read the questions on the *Sentence Analysis* activity sheet aloud.

7. Provide time for students to discuss the questions with their partners. Then, have each student complete the activity sheet.

Fourth Read (Point of View)

1. Read the first sentence of the text aloud. It says: "Many people have called Hatshepsut the greatest woman in Egypt's history." Ask, "What does this opening sentence tell us about the author's point of view and the purpose of this text?" Guide students in a class discussion.

2. Tell the students that you want them to look closely at the way the author chose to portray Hatshepsut. Have students reread the text sections titled "An Empty Throne" and "The Power Behind the Throne" again. Ask them to highlight portions of the text that directly describe Hatshepsut.

3. Display the *Hatshepsut: The Female Pharaoh* text (page 63) using a projector or document camera. Ask students to share the words and phrases that they highlighted in Step 2. Highlight these sections on the projected text.

4. Discuss the author's word choices in the highlighted text sections. Ask, "Do these words sound mainly positive or mainly negative? What tone do these words and phrases set?"

5. Distribute copies of the *Hatshepsut: Patient or Power-Hungry?* activity sheet (page 69) to students. Read the directions aloud.

6. Provide time for students to complete the *Hatshepsut: Patient or Power-Hungry?* activity sheet independently or with partners.

7. Provide time for students to share their responses with the class.

Writing Connection

1. Review the aspects of informational text covered in the close reading activities (descriptions of individuals, text structure, point of view/ purpose).

2. Review various strategies for organizing information when writing informational texts (compare/contrast, description, problem/solution, etc.). Tell students that, for this activity, they will use a cause/effect text structure to explain how Hatshepsut became Egypt's first female pharaoh.

3. Distribute copies of the *Cause and Effect* graphic organizer (page 70) to students. Model how to record one of the causes (*Hatshepsut's two brothers died young*). Remind students to consider both Hatshepsut's characteristics as well as the events that led to her rule.

4. Provide time for students to complete the activity sheet.

5. Place students in small groups to share their responses. Encourage them to add additional causes.

6. Distribute copies of *The Female Pharaoh* activity sheet (page 71) to students. Read the prompt and the directions aloud. Explain to students how they will use their completed *Cause and Effect* graphic organizers to write an explanatory essay.

7. Provide time for students to write the explanatory essay about Hatshepsut's path to power. Display students' completed essays on a classroom bulletin board.

Name: _____ **Date:** _____

Traits of Hatshepsut

Directions: Complete the chart below using adjectives that describe Hatshepsut. Cite evidence from the text to support each adjective.

Adjective	Textual Evidence

Name: _____   **Date:** _____

Sentence Analysis

Directions: Read the sentence below. Answer the questions. Support your answers with evidence from the text.

> *She knew her father must have missed his sons, so she sometimes wore boy's clothing to make him feel better.*

1. How does this sentence fit into the paragraph?

_____

_____

_____

_____

_____

2. How does this sentence fit into the passage as a whole?

_____

_____

_____

_____

_____

Name: _____   **Date:** _____

Hatshepsut: Patient or Power-Hungry?

Directions: Use the text to answer the questions below.

> _In about 1473 bc, Hatshepsut declared herself pharaoh. She took the throne and ruled Egypt for about 22 years. She was well respected. She brought energy and wisdom to Egypt's history. When she died, Thutmose III became the new pharaoh._

1. What is the author's point of view about Hatshepsut's actions?

_____

_____

_____

_____

_____

2. What words or phrases in the text give clues about the author's point of view?

_____

_____

_____

_____

_____

_____

_____

_____

Name: _____   **Date:** _____

Cause and Effect

Directions: How did Hatshepsut become Egypt's first female pharaoh? Go back to the text to examine the causes of Hatshepsut's rise to power. List them on the chart below.

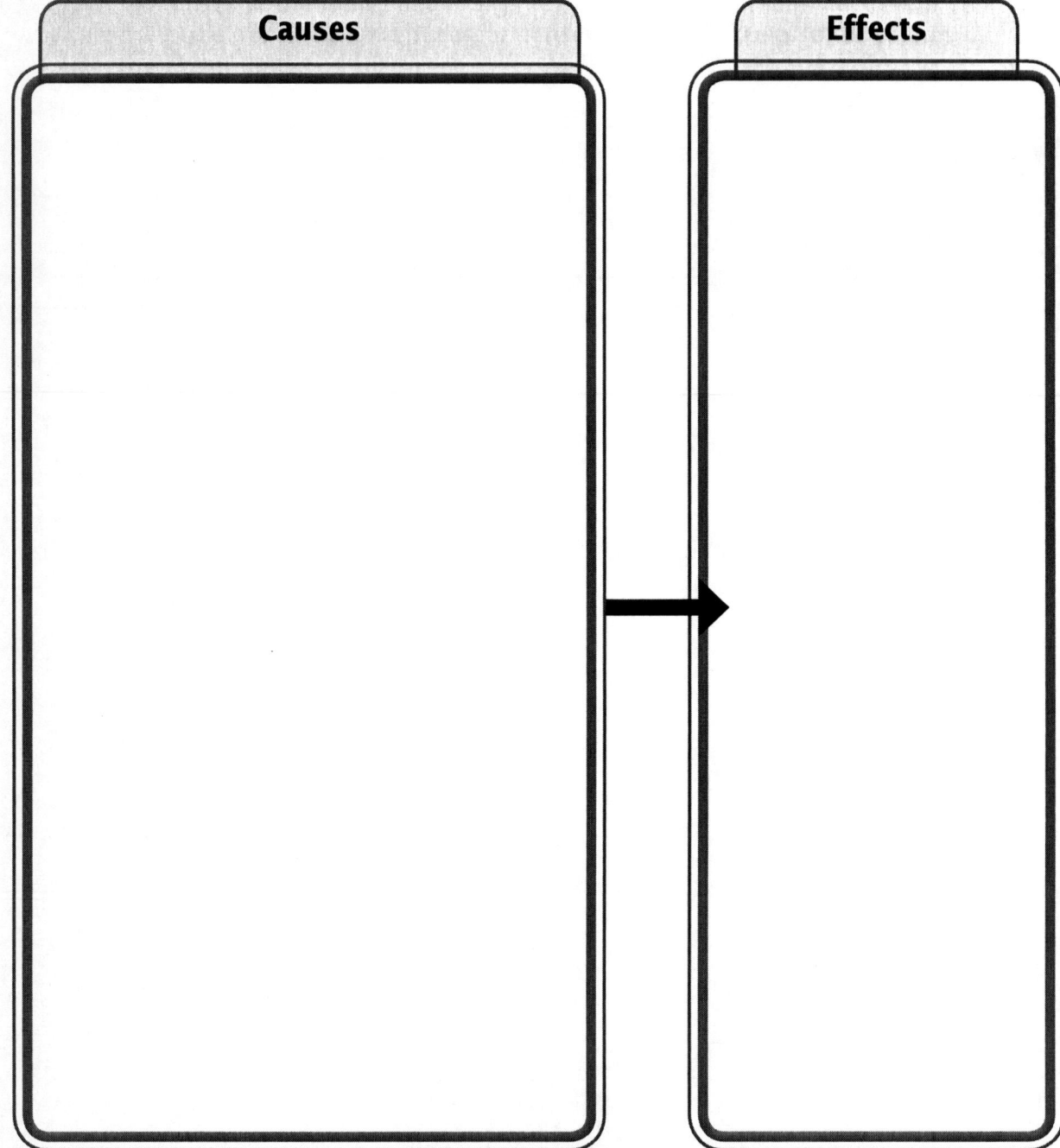

Causes	Effects

   #51505—Connect to Text: Strategies for Close Reading and Writing

Name: _____ **Date:** _____

The Female Pharaoh

Directions: Explain in your own words how Hatshepsut became Egypt's first female pharaoh. Use the chart from the *Cause and Effect* activity sheet to help you organize your ideas. Remember to refer to the text for specific words, phrases, and evidence to support your ideas.

_____

_____

_____

_____

_____

_____

_____

_____

_____

_____

_____

_____

_____

_____

_____

_____

_____

_____

_____

The United States Bill of Rights

Standards

- Cite strong and thorough textual evidence to support analysis of what the text says explicitly as well as inferences drawn from the text, including determining where the text leaves matters uncertain.

- Determine two or more central ideas of a text and analyze their development over the course of the text, including how they interact and build on one another to provide a complex analysis; provide an objective summary of the text.

- Determine the meaning of words and phrases as they are used in a text, including figurative, connotative, and technical meanings; analyze how an author uses and refines the meaning of a key term or terms over the course of a text.

- Analyze seventeenth-, eighteenth-, and nineteenth-century foundational US documents of historical and literary significance for their themes, purposes, and rhetorical features.

- Develop the topic thoroughly by selecting the most significant and relevant facts, extended definitions, concrete details, quotations, or other information and examples appropriate to the audience's knowledge of the topic.

Overview

The United States Bill of Rights is an important document that has substantial historical and political significance in both American history and current events. However, the legal terminology, complex sentence structure, and theoretical concepts make this text difficult to comprehend. In this lesson, students ask questions, note unknown words and confusing concepts, and summarize the amendments. Students then analyze the text to identify ideas stated explicitly, ideas that can be inferred, and ideas that are open to interpretation. Finally, students examine the broader themes and concepts of the Bill of Rights. In the writing connection activity, students apply what they have learned to write an informational text that analyzes the similarities and differences among the major themes of the document.

Areas of Focus

- summarizing

- inferences

- theme

Materials

- *The United States Bill of Rights* (page 73)

- *Bill of Rights Summary* (page 77)

- *Inferences and Uncertainties* (page 78)

- *Analyzing the Bill of Rights* (page 79)

- projector or document camera

- dictionaries

- chart paper

The United States Bill of Rights

I. Congress shall make no law respecting an establishment of religion, or prohibiting the free exercise thereof; or abridging the freedom of speech, or of the press, or the right of the people peaceably to assemble, and to petition the Government for a redress of grievances.

II. A well-regulated militia, being necessary to the security of a free State, the right of the people to keep and bear arms, shall not be infringed.

III. No soldier shall, in time of peace be quartered in any house, without the consent of the owner, nor in time of war, but in a manner to be prescribed by law.

IV. The right of the people to be secure in their persons, houses, papers, and effects, against unreasonable searches and seizures, shall not be violated, and no Warrants shall issue, but upon probable cause, supported by oath or affirmation, and particularly describing the place to be searched, and the persons or things to be seized.

V. No person shall be held to answer for a capital, or otherwise infamous crime, unless on a presentment or indictment of a Grand Jury, except in cases arising in the land or naval forces, or in the Militia, when in actual service in time of War or public danger; nor shall any person be subject for the same offense to be twice put in jeopardy of life or limb; nor shall be compelled in any criminal case to be a witness against himself, nor be deprived of life, liberty, or property, without due process of law; nor shall private property be taken for public use without just compensation.

VI. In all criminal prosecutions, the accused shall enjoy the right to a speedy and public trial, by an impartial jury of the State and district wherein the crime shall have been committed, which district shall have been previously ascertained by law, and to be informed of the nature and cause of the accusation; to be confronted with the witnesses against him; to have compulsory process for obtaining witnesses in his favor, and to have the assistance of counsel for his defense.

VII. In suits at common law, where the value in controversy shall exceed twenty dollars, the right of trial by jury shall be preserved, and no fact tried by a jury shall be otherwise re-examined in any court of the United States, than according to the rules of the common law.

VIII. Excessive bail shall not be required nor excessive fines imposed, nor cruel and unusual punishments inflicted.

IX. The enumeration in the Constitution, of certain rights, shall not be construed to deny or disparage others retained by the people.

X. The powers not delegated to the United States by the Constitution, nor prohibited by it to the States, are reserved to the States respectively, or to the people.

Close Reading Activities

First Read (Overview/First Impressions)

1. Distribute copies of *The United States Bill of Rights* text (page 73) to students.

2. Call students' attention to the numbers next to each paragraph in the passage in the left margin. Explain that they should refer to these numbers when quoting from the text.

3. Before reading, remind students that the first read is to help them gather their initial impressions of the text. Remind them to note the following on the text using the suggested marks:

   - questions about the text (?) (write question in the margin)
   - words or phrases they want to learn more about (put box around)
   - words or phrases that seem important (*)
   - areas of interest or confusion (!)
   - related ideas or concepts (⟳) (write connection in the margin)

4. Read the text aloud. *The Bill of Rights* contains legal terminology and other formal language, so it is helpful for students to hear it read aloud at least once.

5. Provide time for students to revisit their notes and make additional annotations on the text.

6. Use a projector or document camera to display the text. Invite students to discuss their questions, thoughts, and areas of confusion. Demonstrate how to record these ideas on the text.

Second Read (Summarizing)

1. Place students in 10 groups. Assign each group one amendment.

2. Ask students to reread their assigned amendments with their groups. Have them review the text to find any unknown or confusing words or important words or phrases that they previously marked during the first read.

3. Ask students to use dictionaries, context clues, and other resources to determine the meanings of unknown or confusing words and phrases.

4. Distribute copies of the *Bill of Rights Summary* activity sheet (page 77) to students. Have students work with their groups to summarize their amendments in their own words.

5. Display the *Bill of Rights Summary* activity sheet using a projector or document camera. Ask one representative from each group to read the summary aloud. Record each summary on the activity sheet. Have students record the summary of each amendment on their own activity sheets.

Third Read (Inferences)

1. Display the first amendment using a projector or document camera. Have students reread the first part of the first amendment, *"Congress shall make no law respecting an establishment of religion, or prohibiting the free exercise thereof...."*

2. Ask students to restate that phrase in their own words to a classmate sitting nearby.

3. Underline the phrase, *"...make no law respecting an establishment of religion...."* Point out that "establishment" can be a verb meaning the action of starting something. It can also be a noun referring to an organization or institution. Ask, "How might these two meanings of the word 'establishment' influence the way this part of the amendment is interpreted?" Guide students in a class discussion.

4. Display the *Inferences and Uncertainties* activity sheet (page 78) using a projector or document camera. Using the first amendment as an example, model how to record the amendment number, the details stated in the text, the details that can be inferred, and the areas of uncertainty in the text.

5. Place students in nine groups and assign each group an amendment (excluding the first amendment since it was used as an example). Have students work independently to complete the *Inferences and Uncertainties* activity sheet.

6. After students have completed the activity sheet, have groups discuss their responses. Remind students to refer back to the text for evidence to support their answers during the discussion.

7. Provide time for groups to present their data. Record the information on a sheet of chart paper.

8. Ask, "How do the inferences and areas of uncertainty affect the interpretation of the Bill of Rights?" Explain how these areas of ambiguity have led to many current political debates. For example, the modern-day death penalty debate stems from the uncertainty about the phrase "cruel and unusual punishment."

Fourth Read (Theme)

1. Display the *Bill of Rights* using a projector or a document camera. On chart paper, write the amendment numbers I–X down the left side of the paper.

2. Read the first amendment aloud to the class. Have students review their summaries of this amendment from the completed *Bill of Rights Summary* activity sheets. Ask, "What are the major themes of this amendment?" Record their responses.

3. Repeat the procedure for the other amendments.

4. Ask, "What broader categories do these themes represent?" Guide them to the categories of privacy, security, protection from government domination, personal freedom, etc. Discuss how these categories are related.

Writing Connection

1. Review the aspects of informational text covered in the close reading activities (word meaning, theme, analyzing inferences, etc.).

2. Distribute copies of the *Analyzing the Bill of Rights* activity sheet (page 79) to students.

3. Read the directions aloud. Remind students to refer back to the text for evidence, examples, and specific words and phrases to support their ideas. Encourage them to include details, quotations, and significant facts from the text.

4. Have students complete the writing activity on the *Analyzing the Bill of Rights* activity sheet.

5. Display students' written responses on a classroom bulletin board. This writing exercise may also be used as the basis for an extended research project and writing assignment on the Bill of Rights.

Name: _____ **Date:** _____

Bill of Rights Summary

Directions: Reread your assigned amendment. Using your own words, write an objective summary of the amendment in the appropriate box. Record your classmates' summaries of the other amendments.

Amendment	Objective Summary
I	
II	
III	
IV	
V	
VI	
VII	
VIII	
IX	
X	

Name: _____   **Date:** _____

Inferences and Uncertainties

Directions: Reread your assigned amendment. In the chart below, record the amendment number. Then, categorize the details about the amendment according to how they were conveyed in the text: details stated in the text, details inferred from the text, and areas of uncertainty.

Amendment Number	Details Stated in the Text	Details Inferred from the Text	Areas of Uncertainty

Name: _____ **Date:** _____

Analyzing the Bill of Rights

Directions: Respond to the writing prompt below. Remember to include specific details, words, facts, quotations, and evidence from the Bill of Rights to support your response.

> Analyze at least three major themes in the Bill of Rights. How do these themes support a unifying purpose? How do they conflict?

_____

_____

_____

_____

_____

_____

_____

_____

_____

_____

_____

_____

_____

_____

_____

_____

_____

_____

_____

#51505—*Connect to Text: Strategies for Close Reading and Writing* © *Shell Education*

Connect to Opinion/Argument Text

As soon as they begin to speak, children learn to express their desires and opinions. They negotiate for later bedtimes, extra desserts, and the exclusive use of a favorite toy. They communicate their opinions about food, activities, and relationships. They often try to exert control over the decisions in their lives by using persuasive argument techniques on their parents and peers. As they grow and mature, children learn to express their arguments and opinions in the form of written text as well. Opinion/argument texts have a wide variety of formats and applications in our daily lives.

What Is Opinion/Argument Text?

An opinion/argument text is one that attempts to convince or persuade readers. These texts generally express opinions or arguments and provide supporting reasons and evidence. Opinion/argument texts come in many forms, including letters, speeches, and editorial columns. These texts express opinions, communicate claims, and market products. For example, politicians write opinion speeches to persuade constituents to vote for them. Companies write advertisements to convince consumers to buy their products. All arguments share one main objective—to convince people to believe the viewpoints expressed by the author or speaker.

There are three types of opinion/argument texts: exposition, response, and discussion, according to Keir (2009, 8). Exposition refers to texts that present arguments and supporting reasons or evidence about one side of a question or issue without acknowledging opposing viewpoints. Response texts analyze and evaluate specific events or objects, such as performances, artwork, literary texts, etc. These texts provide opinionated reviews and evaluations, along with recommendations. Discussion texts address both sides of an issue or debate and include reasons and evidence supporting both viewpoints. After weighing both sides of an issue, discussion texts often give an opinion favoring one side over the other.

Opinion/Argument Text and Today's Standards

The College and Career Readiness Standards for Reading list the skills for reading opinion/argument texts under the category of Integration of Knowledge and Ideas. Anchor Standard 8 says students should be able to, "Delineate and evaluate the argument and specific claims in a text, including the validity of the reasoning as well as the relevance and sufficiency of the evidence" (NGA and CCSSO 2010a). This standard only applies to reading informational text. It does not apply to reading literature.

The College and Career Readiness Standards for Writing outline three text types and purposes for student writing. Opinions/arguments are one of these types, along with informative/explanatory texts and narratives. As a distinct category of writing, arguments require specific skills and knowledge. Students must learn and practice these skills in order to produce clear and coherent arguments.

Close Reading and Opinion/Argument Text

Identifying and Describing Reasoning

In the elementary grades, close reading activities for opinion/argument texts teach students to identify and describe an author's line of reasoning. Students learn to recognize the author's main points and isolate the reasons that support each point. Through close reading activities, students analyze specific sentences and paragraphs in texts to determine their purposes and relationships to the author's reasons. Close reading also helps students see how claims and reasons impact arguments. By dissecting arguments and identifying supporting reasons for each point, students learn how authors use language and text structure to write effective opinion/argument texts.

Evaluating Arguments

Middle school students move beyond identifying and describing claims and reasons in argument texts to evaluating arguments. In order to evaluate arguments, students must trace the claims authors make to their reasons and evidence. They must use critical-thinking skills to determine whether the reasons are logical and the evidence is valid. Close reading activities at this level are designed to help students distill the main points and reasons from the text and analyze their validity.

Evidence

Perhaps the most challenging aspect of analyzing argument texts is evaluating the author's supporting evidence. By definition, opinion/argument texts are designed to convince or persuade readers. Students who are college and career ready are able to accurately assess the validity of the arguments they encounter, from TV commercials to America's founding documents. In order to evaluate the effectiveness of arguments, students must determine if the supporting evidence is relevant and sufficient. Close reading activities at the high school level help students differentiate between relevant and irrelevant evidence in texts, identify false or inaccurate claims, and assess the credibility of sources.

Writing Opinion/Argument Text

The close reading of opinion/argument texts improves students' writing skills, as well as their reading comprehension skills. After reading and analyzing a variety of argument texts, students recognize the difference between effective and ineffective arguments. They learn the importance of clearly stated claims, supporting reasons, and valid evidence.

Mentor texts also expose students to different formats and styles of argument texts. While some argument texts present only one side of a debate, other texts address both sides. Students learn to anticipate readers' reactions to claims and address possible concerns and biases up front. They internalize the importance of maintaining a formal style and objective tone when writing argument texts. They also see the powerful impact made by strong concluding statements. Close reading not only enhances the reciprocal relationship between reading and writing, but it also facilitates a deeper understanding of the elements that make opinion/argument texts effective and convincing.

Text-Dependent Questions and Prompts to Support Close Reading and Writing of Opinion/Argument Texts

The following text-dependent questions and prompts cover some of the broad areas of focus in literacy. When planning close reading and writing activities, these questions and prompts should be tailored to fit the selected text passages.

Identifying and Describing Reasoning

- What is the author trying to tell the reader? What specific reasons does he/she give to support this point in the text?

- How many reasons does the author provide to support his/her claim that _____? Describe each reason.

- Why does the author claim _____ in the text? Support your answer with evidence from the text.

- What is the author's opinion about _____? How do you know?

Evaluating Arguments

- Which claims in the text are supported by reasons? Which are not?

- Does the author use sound reasoning to support his/her claim that _____? Justify your answer with support from the text.

- Does the author make any claims that are not supported by reasons or evidence? If so, which ones?

- Evaluate the effectiveness of the author's claim. Support your opinion with examples from the text.

- Are the main points in the text sufficiently supported with reasons and evidence? Provide examples to support your answer.

Evidence

- What evidence does the author provide to support the point that _____?

- Evaluate the evidence presented to support the argument that _____. Is the evidence relevant?

- How does the author validate his/her claim in the text? Is this evidence sufficient? Be sure to refer to the text in your answer.

- What sources does the author use to provide evidence in support of his/her claim? Are these sources credible? Why or why not?

- Does the text include any irrelevant evidence? Be sure to include examples from the text in your response.

- Do you trust the reasoning behind the author's argument/claim? What elements of the text make you feel this way?

The Best Job

Overview

Primary students often struggle to differentiate between fact and opinion. In this lesson, students gather their initial impressions of the text and then find opinion statements in the text. In the second close reading activity, students ask questions about key details. The third close reading activity guides students to make connections among text details. The final close reading activity helps students explain how the reasons in the text support the opinion statement. For the writing connection, students write an opinion piece about what they want to be when they grow up.

Standards

- Ask and answer questions about key details in a text.
- Describe the connection between two individuals, events, ideas, or pieces of information in a text.
- Identify the reasons an author gives to support points in a text.
- Write opinion pieces in which they introduce the topic or name the book they are writing about, state an opinion, supply a reason for the opinion, and provide some sense of closure.

Areas of Focus

- key details
- connecting information
- reasoning
- stating opinions

Materials

- *The Best Job* (page 86)
- *Fact vs. Opinion* (page 90)
- *Connecting Sentences* (page 91)
- *My Perfect Job* (page 92)
- *When I Grow Up...* (page 93)
- projector or document camera
- puppet or stuffed animal
- chart paper
- coloring supplies
- Author's Chair (*optional*)

The Best Job

I want to be a doctor. It is the best job!

Doctors help. They give medicine. They teach healthy habits. They find cures.

Doctors work with different people. Doctors help kids. They help adults, too.

Doctors work in many places. Some work in hospitals. Others work in clinics.

It is fun to be a doctor.

#51505—Connect to Text: Strategies for Close Reading and Writing

Close Reading Activities

First Read (Overview/First Impressions)

1. Use a projector or document camera to display *The Best Job* (page 86).

2. Ask students to imagine that a classroom puppet or stuffed animal is the author of the text. Explain that the animal is going to read his or her nonfiction text aloud. Remind them that nonfiction means *not fake*, or true. This is an informational text written to give information about a topic.

3. Read the text aloud using a different voice to represent the puppet talking. Use your finger or a pointer to track the print.

4. Ask students to share their initial impressions of the text with the puppet. Respond to their comments using the puppet's voice. Ask, "Can you think of questions you would like to ask _____ (name of puppet or stuffed animal) about the text?" Encourage students to ask the puppet questions about unfamiliar words and confusing ideas. Have the puppet or stuffed animal answer the questions. Discuss the text as a class.

Second Read (Key Details)

1. Tell students that a fact is a true piece of information. Give examples that will make sense to your students. (*The carpet is blue. We have 21 students in this class. Ryan is a boy. Sierra is a girl.*) Explain that an opinion is a person's own belief or idea about something. Give examples that match students' own opinions to reinforce the idea that opinions are personal. (*Broccoli is yummy. Orange is the prettiest color. Fish are the best pets.*)

2. Ask students to listen for an opinion statement in the text. Have students read along as you read the text aloud again.

3. Ask, "Which sentence states the author's opinion?" Underline the sentence, *It is the best job*. Talk about why this is an opinion and not a fact.

4. Distribute copies of the *Fact vs. Opinion* activity sheet (page 90) to students. Explain that they will need to differentiate between factual statements and opinion statements on the activity sheet. Tell them that they should ask themselves the question, "Is it possible that someone might not agree with this statement?" to differentiate between fact and opinion. If the answer is yes, then the statement is most likely an opinion.

5. Provide time for students to complete the activity sheet independently.

6. Review the activity sheet as a class. For every statement, ask the question, "Is it possible that someone might not agree with this statement?" Think aloud as you explain whether each statement is a fact or an opinion.

Third Read (Connecting Information)

1. Display a copy of the *The Best Job* text (page 86) using a projector or document camera. Have students read the text chorally.

2. Reread the first two sentences aloud. Ask, "What is the connection between these two sentences?" Help students understand that the opinion in the second sentence explains *why* the author wants to be a doctor. Draw an arrow between the two sentences to show the connection.

3. Read the third sentence ("Doctors help.") aloud to the class. Help students understand how the third sentence provides support for the opinion in the previous sentence. Then, guide them to see how the sentence that follows it ("They give medicine.") is an example of how doctors help. Draw arrows between the third sentence and the sentences before and after it to show the connections.

4. Display the *Connecting Sentences* activity sheet (page 91) using a projector or document camera. Read the sentences on the activity sheet aloud to the class. Demonstrate how to draw a line between the related sentences.

5. Provide time for students to complete the activity sheet independently.

6. Review the answers on the activity sheet as a class. Have students make corrections as needed.

Fourth Read (Reasoning)

1. Explain to the class that a well-written opinion piece always gives reasons that explain the author's opinion.

2. Display the text using a projector or document camera. Review the author's opinion. At the top of a piece of chart paper, write the opinion statement, "Being a doctor is the best job." Ask students to identify the reasons that explain the author's opinion.

3. Reread the first three sentences. Ask students to read to find out why the author wants to be a doctor. Once students have read and shared their thoughts, on the chart paper, write the supporting reason, "Doctors help people."

4. Have students identify the next reason in the text, "Doctors work with different people." Explain that it is the author's opinion that it would be fun to work with kids and adults.

5. Have students identify the third supporting reason, "Doctors work in many places." Explain that it is the author's opinion that it would be fun to work in hospitals and clinics.

6. Distribute copies of the *My Perfect Job* activity sheet (page 92) to students. Use a projector or document camera to display the activity sheet. Think aloud as you model how to write the name of your perfect job and write three reasons why you think this is the best job.

7. Provide time for students to complete the activity sheet independently.

8. Ask students to share their work with the class. Review how the reasons support each student's opinion.

Writing Connection

1. Distribute copies of *The Best Job* to students. Have students read the text independently. Review how the author stated an opinion and gave supporting reasons.

2. Have students get out their completed *My Perfect Job* activity sheets from the fourth close reading activity. Display your sample activity sheet using a projector or document camera. Review your opinion and supporting reasons and make any necessary revisions. Have students reread their completed activity sheets. Ask them to revise their responses as needed.

3. Display the *When I Grow Up...* activity sheet (page 93) using a document camera or projector. Model how to write a paragraph describing your perfect job with three reasons to support your opinion. Draw an illustration to accompany the opinion essay.

4. Distribute copies of the *When I Grow Up...* activity sheet to students. Provide time for students to complete the writing project independently. Remind them to include an opinion statement, three supporting reasons, and an illustration on a separate sheet of paper.

5. Ask students to come to the front of the class and read their essays. Provide an Author's Chair for the students to sit in while they read their paragraphs and display their illustrations. Post their work on a bulletin board.

Name: _____ **Date:** _____

Fact vs. Opinion

Directions: Read each statement. Circle "fact" or "opinion."

> **Example:** Being a doctor is the best job.
>
> Fact   **Opinion**

1. Doctors work with different types of people.

   Fact   **Opinion**

2. Going to the doctor is fun!

   Fact   **Opinion**

3. Doctors can give people medicine.

   Fact   **Opinion**

4. Doctors help keep people healthy.

   Fact   **Opinion**

5. Everyone should be a doctor.

   Fact   **Opinion**

Connecting Sentences

Directions: Draw a line between the related sentences. Circle the sentences that tell opinions.

Owls are cool!

Soccer is fun.

Fire is scary.

Spring is the best season.

Flowers bloom in spring.

Owls have three eyelids.

Lots of kids play soccer.

Fire is very hot.

Plums taste better than candy.

Plums are sweet and juicy.

Name: _____ **Date:** _____

My Perfect Job

Directions: Write the job you would like to have when you grow up. Give three reasons why this job would be the best for you.

Name of job: _____

_____

Reason #1: _____

_____

_____

_____

Reason #2: _____

_____

_____

_____

Reason #3: _____

_____

_____

_____

Name: _____ **Date:** _____

When I Grow Up...

Directions: What do you want to be when you grow up? Write your opinion about the best job. Give three reasons that tell why you like the job. End with a conclusion that states your opinion again.

_____

_____

_____

_____

_____

_____

_____

_____

_____

_____

_____

_____

_____

_____

_____

_____

_____

_____

The Birthday Wish

Standards

- Ask and answer questions to demonstrate understanding of a text, referring explicitly to the text as the basis for the answers.

- Distinguish their own point of view from that of the author of a text.

- Describe the logical connection between particular sentences and paragraphs in a text.

- Introduce the topic or text they are writing about, state an opinion, and create an organizational structure that lists reasons.

Overview

This text provides an ideal platform to explore the role point of view plays in opinion texts. After gathering their initial impressions, students examine the opinions in the text and discuss the implied counter opinion. Students then design questions to address these. The next close reading activity adds another layer of comprehension by helping students differentiate between three different points of view: the narrator's, the parents' (inferred), and their own. In the final close reading activity, students analyze the purpose of each paragraph and determine how each paragraph builds on the previous ones to construct a cohesive opinion. In the writing connection activity, students use their knowledge gained through the close reading activities to write their own opinion piece about a similar topic. For the writing connection, students use the text passage as a mentor text to help them structure and organize an opinion essay.

Areas of Focus

- asking questions
- point of view
- text structure
- organizing opinions

Materials

- *The Birthday Wish* (page 95)
- *Questioning the Wish* (page 99)
- *Point of View* (page 100)
- *Paragraph Structure* (page 101)
- *Organizing an Opinion* (page 102)
- *My Birthday Wish* (page 103)
- projector or document camera
- chart paper

The Birthday Wish

Tomorrow is my birthday, and I will be nine years old. I only want one thing for my birthday: a pet. I want a guinea pig. My parents say I am not ready, but I know I am.

Pets can be a lot of work. I know this because I did some research at the library on guinea pigs. I learned that long-haired guinea pigs need their hair brushed every day so that it doesn't get tangled. Short-haired guinea pigs are easier. You do not need to brush their hair. I would like to get a short-haired guinea pig.

I also went to the pet store to learn more about guinea pigs. I talked to someone who worked in the store. She told me that guinea pigs need fresh food and water every day. They need to have their cages cleaned when they get messy. Guinea pigs need someone to play with them so they do not get lonely.

I believe I am ready to have my own pet. I am very responsible. Every morning I get myself ready for school. I get dressed, brush my teeth and my hair, and pack my backpack. I know how to get myself breakfast and rinse my dishes when I am done. I also help take care of my little brother. I walk him to school in the mornings and pick him up after school. I help him tie his shoes and button his jacket.

I really hope I get a guinea pig for my birthday. I am responsible and ready for the commitment!

Close Reading Activities

First Read (Overview/First Impressions)

1. Distribute copies of *The Birthday Wish* text (page 95) to students.

2. Use a projector or document camera to display the text. Demonstrate how to number each line of the passage on the left side of the text. Have students number their copies. Explain that they should refer to these numbers when quoting from the text.

3. Before reading, remind students that the first read is to help them gather their initial impressions of the text. Remind them to note the following on the text using the suggested marks:

   - questions about the text (?) (write question in the margin)

   - words or phrases they want to learn more about (put box around)

   - words or phrases that seem important (*)

   - areas of interest or confusion (!)

4. Read the text aloud to the class as students follow along.

5. After the initial reading is complete, provide time for students to revisit their notes and make additional annotations on the text.

6. Use a projector or document camera to display the text. Invite students to discuss their questions, thoughts, and areas of confusion. Demonstrate how to record these ideas on the text.

Second Read (Asking Questions)

1. Have students read the text aloud with partners.

2. Ask, "Why might the narrator's parents not want their child to get a pet?" Discuss the counterarguments parents might have against a pet. List these on chart paper.

3. Ask students to pretend that they are the narrator's parents. Ask, "As a parent, what questions would you ask your child before agreeing to get a pet?" Give an example, such as, *"Will you have time to care for a pet?"*

4. Distribute the *Questioning the Wish* activity sheet (page 99). Provide time for students to complete the activity sheet independently.

5. Place students in pairs. Have partners act out a conversation between the author and a parent. Each student should have a chance to play the parent and ask the questions on the activity sheet. When playing the part of the author, students should refer to the text as the basis for their answers.

6. After completing the role-play activity, ask volunteers to share their questions and answers. Reinforce the importance of referencing the text in the questions and answers.

#51505—Connect to Text: Strategies for Close Reading and Writing   © Shell Education

Third Read (Point of View)

1. Have students reread the text independently.

2. Display a copy of the text using a projector or document camera. Ask, "Who is telling this story? How do you know?" Discuss that a nameless narrator is telling this story about himself or herself. Say, "We will call this narrator the author."

3. Ask, "What is the author's point of view or opinion on the subject of getting a pet?" Have students support their responses with words and sentences from the text that show the author's point of view.

4. Distribute copies of the *Point of View* activity sheet (page 100) to students. Using a projector or document camera, display the activity sheet. Think aloud as you make notes about the narrator's point of view. Then, refer to the text as you demonstrate how to record specific phrases and sentences that convey this point of view.

5. Place students with partners. Have students complete the first two rows of the chart with their partners. Remind students that the parents' point of view must be inferred.

6. Provide time for students to share responses with the class.

7. Direct the students' attention to the last row of the chart. Explain that they will explain their own points of view about getting a guinea pig. Discuss how this point of view may be the same as the author's or it may be different. Have students note specific words and phrases in the text that they strongly agree or disagree with. These agreements and disagreements help differentiate between the author's point of view and the readers' points of view.

8. Have students complete the activity sheet with partners. Provide time for volunteers to share their responses with the class.

Fourth Read (Text Structure)

1. Tell students that the structure of an essay is much like the structure of a house. The structure of a house is the framing and rafters that hold it together. You cannot see the structure beneath the finished product, but it is there inside the walls and ceiling. Explain that the structure of a text refers to the way the ideas are put together. It takes some digging to see the structure of an essay, but it is holding the text together.

2. Explain that structure is key to the effectiveness of arguments. Tell students that they will examine the structure of the text to see how it helps convey the author's argument.

3. Distribute copies of the *Paragraph Structure* activity sheet (page 101) to students.

4. Display a copy of the text using a projector or document camera. Read the first paragraph aloud. Ask, "Why did the author write this paragraph?" Help students see that the author uses this paragraph to introduce the issue and to state his or her point of view.

5. Model how to underline the specific parts of the paragraph that convey the purpose. Demonstrate how to annotate the text to note the significance of the underlined sentences. Remind students to take notes on their activity sheets.

6. Repeat Step 5 with the remaining paragraphs.

7. Review the purpose of each paragraph with the class and discuss how the paragraphs are connected. Analyze how each paragraph contributes to the overall argument.

Writing Connection

1. Review the structure of the opinions in *The Birthday Wish*. Tell students that they will use the text passage as a mentor text to write their own opinion text.

2. Ask students to think of a birthday wish of their own.

3. Distribute copies of the *Organizing an Opinion* activity sheet (page 102) to students. Have them complete the activity sheet independently. Remind students to refer back to the mentor text to get ideas about how to organize their own opinions.

4. Distribute copies of the *My Birthday Wish* activity sheet (page 103) to students. Provide time for them to write their own opinions.

5. Have each student read his or her opinion aloud to a partner. Encourage students to give their partners two compliments and one suggestion for improvement.

Name: _____ **Date:** _____

Questioning the Wish

Directions: Imagine you are the parent of the author. What questions do you have for the author before granting the birthday wish?

1. _____

_____

_____

2. _____

_____

_____

3. _____

_____

_____

Name: _____ **Date:** _____

Point of View

Directions: Describe the three points of view on the chart below. Write down the words and phrases from the text that made that point of view clear.

Point of View	Textual Evidence or Support
Narrator:	
Parents:	
You:	

Name: _____ **Date:** _____

Paragraph Structure

Directions: Answer the questions below to determine the purpose of each paragraph.

Why did the author write paragraph #1?

_____

_____

_____

Why did the author write paragraph #2?

_____

_____

_____

Why did the author write paragraph #3?

_____

_____

_____

Why did the author write paragraph #4?

_____

_____

_____

Why did the author write paragraph #5?

_____

_____

_____

Name: _____ **Date:** _____

Organizing an Opinion

Directions: Use the graphic organizer to plan an opinion for your birthday wish.

Opinion Statement: _____

_____

Reason #1: _____

_____

_____

Reason #2: _____

_____

_____

Reason #3: _____

_____

_____

Conclusion: _____

_____

_____

#51505—*Connect to Text: Strategies for Close Reading and Writing* © *Shell Education*

Name: _____ **Date:** _____

My Birthday Wish

Directions: Use the outline from *Organizing an Opinion* to write your opinion on the lines below.

_____

_____

_____

_____

_____

_____

_____

_____

_____

_____

Let's Have Year-Round School

Standards

- Describe the overall structure of events, ideas, concepts, or information in a text or part of a text.
- Interpret information presented visually, orally, or quantitatively and explain how the information contributes to an understanding of the text in which it appears.
- Explain how an author uses reasons and evidence to support particular points in a text.
- Link opinion and reasons using words and phrases.

Overview

This text passage provides the opportunity for students to examine opinions about traditional vs. year-round school calendars. Students analyze how the author presents these opinions by examining text structure, visual media, and the author's reasoning. After gathering their initial impressions, students identify the purpose of each paragraph. They then analyze the text structure to compare the two types of calendars. In the third close reading activity, students analyze the visual information to determine how it supports the text. The final close reading activity helps students identify the main opinions and examine the supporting reasons. For the writing connection, students write their own opinion piece arguing the other side of the debate: traditional school calendars are better than year-round calendars.

Areas of Focus

- text structure
- visual media
- reasoning
- linking reasons

Materials

- *Let's Have Year-Round School* (page 105)
- *Comparing Calendars* (page 109)
- *School Calendars* (page 110)
- *Opinions and Reasons* (page 111)
- *Outline of an Opinion* (page 112)
- *Siding with Tradition* (page 113)
- projector or document camera
- chart paper
- four different colored markers (per student)

Let's Have Year-Round School

Summer vacation is too long. Students forget important lessons over the summer. They have to review everything when they come back to school and readjust to the school schedule.

The traditional school year calendar was created when many people lived on farms. Students had the summer off so they could help with the harvesting. Today, most people do not live on farms. They do not need the whole summer off.

The traditional schedule is hard for families where both parents work outside the home. Working parents do not get summer vacation. Instead, they have to find someone to take care of their children. This change in schedule can disrupt people's lives. Then, just when everyone gets used to the new schedule, it is time to go back to school. That means everyone has to revert back to the school schedule. These types of changes can be hard for families.

I propose that there should be more year-round schools. In this model, school vacations happen throughout the year. Students are still in school for the same amount of time. The vacation schedule is just spread out throughout the year. Instead of two months off in the summer, there may be only one month off. Students could still go to summer camp and have a summer vacation. Students and teachers would feel less burned out during the school year because vacations would be spread out.

The research is mixed about whether year-round schools improve student achievement. Some students show improvement whereas others do not. Despite this, I still think the year-round school is a better model.

Comparing Sample School Calendars

	Jan.	Feb.	Mar.	Apr.	May	June	July	Aug.	Sept.	Oct.	Nov.	Dec.
Traditional Calendar	X	X	X	X	X	–	–	–	X	X	X	X
Year-Round Calendar	X	X	–	X	X	X	–	X	X	X	–	X

X = school in session   – = vacation

Close Reading Activities

First Read (Overview/First Impressions)

1. Distribute copies of the *Let's Have Year-Round School* text (page 105) to students.

2. Use a projector or document camera to display the text. Demonstrate how to number each line of the passage on the left side of the text. Have students number their copies. Explain that they should refer to these numbers when quoting from the text.

3. Before reading, remind students that the first read is to help them gather their initial impressions of the text. Remind them to note the following on the text using the suggested marks:

   • questions about the text (?) (write question in the margin)

   • words or phrases they want to learn more about (put box around)

   • words or phrases that seem important (*)

   • areas of interest or confusion (!)

   • related ideas or concepts (⬭) (write connection in the margin)

   • areas of agreement or disagreement (△ = agree ▽= disagree)

4. Have students read the text independently.

5. After the initial reading is complete, provide time for students to revisit their notes and make additional annotations on the text.

6. Use a projector or document camera to display the text passage. Have students share their questions, thoughts, and areas of confusion concerning the text. Demonstrate how to record these ideas on the text passage.

Second Read (Text Structure)

1. Display the text using a projector or document camera. Read the first paragraph aloud.

2. Think aloud as you summarize the first paragraph. Next, model how to record notes about the content in the margin next to the first paragraph. For example, you might write, "Author believes a long summer vacation has a negative impact on students."

3. Have students read the second paragraph independently. Ask students to orally summarize the paragraph. Make notes in the margin.

4. Place students with partners. Have pairs work together to read and summarize the next three paragraphs.

5. Discuss students' summaries as a class. Then, call attention to the text structure. Make sure students see how the first three paragraphs highlight the problems with the traditional school calendar, the fourth paragraph explains the benefits of year-round school, and the fifth paragraph addresses one of the counteropinions and presents a conclusion.

6. Distribute copies of the *Comparing Calendars* activity sheet (page 109) to students. Use a projector or document camera to display the activity sheet. Reread the first paragraph and model how to add information to the chart.

7. Provide time for students to complete the activity sheet independently.

8. Review the opinions the author presents in favor of the year-round school calendar and against the traditional school calendar. Talk about how this text uses a compare and contrast text structure.

Third Read (Visual Media)

1. Ask, "Why do some informational texts include charts, graphs, maps, and other graphics?" Explain that these visuals provide additional details.

2. Display the text using a projector or document camera. Direct students' attention to the chart. Make sure students understand how to read the chart.

3. Distribute copies of the *School Calendars* activity sheet (page 110) to students. Using a projector or document camera, display the activity sheet. Read the directions aloud.

4. Place students with partners. Provide time for pairs to complete the activity sheet.

5. Review the answers as a class. Have volunteers share their responses.

6. Ask, "How else could the author have presented this information? Why do you think the author chose this format?" Discuss how the visual presentation complements the text.

Fourth Read (Reasoning)

1. Write the following paragraph on chart paper: *Summer vacations are too long. These long breaks hurt students' education. It is not necessary to have such a long vacation. It would be better to have several shorter vacations spread out over the school year.* Read the text aloud to the class.

2. Ask, "Does this paragraph make a compelling argument for a year-round school calendar? Why or why not?" Help students understand that supporting reasons make arguments more effective.

3. Distribute copies of the *Opinions and Reasons* activity sheet (page 111) to students along with four different colored markers. Display the activity sheet using a projector or document camera. Read the directions aloud to the class.

4. Have the class reread the first paragraph of the text. Ask, "What point does the author make in this paragraph?" Help students identify the main opinion and record it on the activity sheet. For example, *"The traditional school calendar hurts students' education."*

5. Ask students to identify the reasons that support the opinion. Have them choose one of the markers and highlight the reasons. List the reasons underneath the main opinion on the activity sheet.

6. Explain that each argument and its supporting reasons will be highlighted in the same colors. Place students with partners. Have them work together to complete the activity sheet.

7. Review the main opinions and supporting reasons as a class.

Writing Connection

1. Ask, "Do you think the author of *Let's Have Year-Round School* makes a good argument?" Have students discuss their opinions in small groups.

2. Tell students that no matter what they personally believe, they will write an opinion piece in support of the other side of the issue.

3. Brainstorm opinions and reasons that support the traditional school calendar. List these on chart paper.

4. Distribute copies of the *Outline of an Opinion* activity sheet (page 112) to students. Provide time for students to complete the activity sheet independently.

5. List transition words and phrases *(for instance, for example, in addition to, furthermore, additionally)* on a sheet of chart paper. Explain that these help readers connect the ideas in texts.

6. Distribute copies of the *Siding with Tradition* activity sheet (page 113) to students. Provide time for students to write their own opinions. Remind them to use at least three linking words or phrases from the class chart.

7. Have each student read his or her opinion aloud to a partner. Encourage students to give their partners two compliments and one suggestion for improvement.

Name: _____ **Date:** _____

Comparing Calendars

Directions: Record the opinions from the text in the columns below.

Opinions Against the Traditional School Calendar	Opinions in Support of the Year-Round School Calendar

Name: _____   **Date:** _____

School Calendars

Directions: Answer the questions below using the information from the text.

1. How many months of vacation does the traditional school calendar have?

   _____

   List the vacation months: _____

   _____

   _____

2. How many months of vacation does the year-round school calendar have?

   _____

   List the vacation months: _____

   _____

   _____

3. How does the use of the chart help you understand the text?

   _____

   _____

   _____

Name: _____ **Date:** _____

Opinions and Reasons

Directions: Reread the text one paragraph at a time. Write the main opinion in each paragraph in the Opinions box. Then, list the reasons the author gave to support each opinion in the Reasons box.

Opinions	Reasons
Paragraph 1	
Paragraph 2	
Paragraph 3	
Paragraph 4	
Paragraph 5	

Name: _____ **Date:** _____

Outline of an Opinion

Directions: List three main opinions in support of the traditional school calendar. List at least two reasons to support each opinion.

Opinion #1: _____

_____

_____

Reasons: _____

_____

_____

Opinion #2: _____

_____

_____

Reasons: _____

_____

_____

Opinion #3: _____

_____

_____

Reasons: _____

_____

_____

 #51505—*Connect to Text: Strategies for Close Reading and Writing*

Name: _____ **Date:** _____

Siding with Tradition

Directions: Use your notes from *Outline of an Opinion* to write an opinion piece in support of the traditional school calendar. Include at least three transition words or phrases.

_____

_____

_____

_____

_____

_____

_____

_____

_____

_____

_____

_____

_____

_____

_____

_____

_____

Saving Our National Parks

Overview

In this lesson, students analyze an argument text to understand how the author uses word choice, claims, and reasons to formulate a convincing argument. As students gain a deeper understanding of argument texts, they are ready to explore the nuances that make arguments compelling and credible. In this lesson, they learn how to write objective summaries of a text without including personal thoughts or opinions. They analyze the author's choice of words and use of nonliteral language in the argument. They also identify the reasons and evidence that support each argument and consider the credibility of the sources. For the writing connection, students research an opposing viewpoint and write an argument in response to the text.

Standards

- Determine two or more central ideas in a text and analyze their development over the course of the text; provide an objective summary of the text.

- Determine the meaning of words and phrases as they are used in a text, including figurative, connotative, and technical meanings; analyze the impact of a specific word choice on meaning and tone.

- Trace and evaluate the argument and specific claims in a text, assessing whether reasoning is sound and the evidence is relevant and sufficient to support the claims.

- Support claim(s) with clear reasons and relevant evidence, using accurate, credible sources and demonstrating an understanding of the topic or text.

Areas of Focus

- summarizing

- word meaning

- arguments and claims

- evidence from sources

Materials

- *Saving Our National Parks* (page 115)

- *Objective and Subjective Summaries* (page 119)

- *Language Decoder* (page 120)

- *National Park Claims and Evidence* (page 121)

- *Response Research* (page 122)

- *National Parks Preservation Response* (page 123)

- projector or document camera

- one red marker and one blue marker (per student)

Saving Our National Parks

There is no more beautiful place in the world than Yellowstone National Park—except maybe Denali National Park in Alaska, or Grand Canyon National Park, or maybe the Fire Island National Seashore. The United States National Park System is a treasure that must be preserved. The United States is covered from sea to shining sea with cities and highways and factories. The amount of green area shrinks all the time.

National parks are among the few places where nature is protected. They are places where we can relax and view wildlife in its own element, which allows us to experience what the nation looked like hundreds of years ago, when it was pure and unspoiled. But the United States park system is in grave danger.

Too Many Tourists

A glut of tourists chokes the parks with cars that cause pollution and run over wildlife. For example, at the entrance to Yellowstone Park, rangers have air pumped into their booths because the pollution is so bad!

Many people camp in the parks, and their poorly tended campfires have turned into wildfires, burning thousands of precious acres. Around coastal parks, motorboats harm and scare wildlife, sometimes preventing them from mating. Oil and gas spilling from the boats' motors pollute the water. During the winter, loud snowmobiles destroy the quiet peace of the parks. In addition to noise pollution, they bring air pollution and terrify the animals.

Stop the Sellout

There is another problem that is even more dangerous than tourists. Our park system is being sold piece by piece to the private sector. Some parkland has already been used for development. Soon there may be private housing built on these preserves that were once untouchable. Another catastrophe is opening public lands to oil drilling. Oil drilling can easily damage delicate ecosystems.

Let's Take Action

The solution is clear. The park service must get tough with tourists. Drastically reduce the number of cars allowed into the parks. Cut the number of snowmobiles or disallow them altogether. Forbid motorboats near coastal parks. Sure, some people will be outraged. However, in the end, they will like the results.

We think the US government should keep the parks from being overused and run down. They should also make sure that public lands cannot be sold to private investors. After all, once the parks are gone, we can't get new ones.

Close Reading Activities

First Read (Overview/First Impressions)

1. Distribute copies of the *Saving Our National Parks* text (page 115) to students. Have students number each paragraph in the left margin. Encourage them to refer to these numbers as they reference the text throughout the close reading activities.

2. Before reading, remind students that the first read is to help them gather their initial impressions of the text. Remind them to note the following on the text using the suggested marks:

   - questions about the text (?) (write question in the margin)

   - words or phrases they want to learn more about (put box around)

   - words or phrases that seem important (*)

   - areas of interest or confusion (!)

   - related ideas or concepts (⬭) (write connection in the margin)

   - areas of agreement or disagreement (△ = agree ▽ = disagree)

   - questions about credibility or sources (circle)

3. Have students read the text independently.

4. After the initial reading is complete, provide time for students to revisit their notes and make additional annotations on the text.

5. Use a projector or document camera to display the text. Invite students to discuss their questions, thoughts, and areas of confusion. Encourage students to record these ideas on their copies of the text.

Second Read (Summarizing)

1. Display the text using a projector or document camera. Read the first paragraph aloud.

2. Ask, "What is the central idea of this text?" Have students refer to specific words and sentences in the text to provide support for their responses. On the projected text, highlight the sentence, "The United States National Park System is a treasure that must be preserved."

3. Write *objective* and *subjective* on the board. Explain that objective means unbiased, impartial, and verifiable by facts. Explain that subjective means subject to personal opinions and not verifiable by facts. Argument texts, for example, are subjective because they present opinions.

4. Ask, "What would a subjective summary sound like? What would an objective summary sound like?" Explain that it is important to be able to summarize texts objectively without inserting opinions or judgments.

5. Distribute copies of the *Objective and Subjective Summaries* activity sheet (page 119) to students. Display the activity sheet using a projector or document camera and read the directions aloud.

6. Read the first two sentences in the subjective summary aloud. Then, model how to remove the subjective statements to make the summary objective.

7. Place students with partners. Provide time for pairs to complete the activity sheet.

8. Review students' revisions as a class. Have students make changes as needed.

Third Read (Word Meaning)

1. Display the text using a projector or document camera. Have students review their initial impression notes in the margins. Ask if anyone noted any words that were either confusing or interesting in the text. Highlight these words on the projected text.

2. Read the first paragraph aloud. Underline, "The United States is covered from sea to shining sea with cities and highways and factories." Ask the class to explain the literal interpretation of this sentence. Then, have students describe the figurative meaning of this sentence. Discuss the purpose of this sentence and why the author chose to use this example of figurative language.

3. Distribute copies of the *Language Decoder* activity sheet (page 120) to students. Have them record the sentence from Step 2, along with the literal and figurative meanings.

4. Place students in groups of 3 or 4 to complete the activity sheet.

5. Have a volunteer from each group share the group's responses with the class. On the projected text, underline the examples of nonliteral language and discuss their impact on the argument.

Fourth Read (Arguments and Claims)

1. Display the text passage using a projector or document camera. Give each student a clean copy of the text. Give each student one red marker and one blue marker.

2. Ask, "What are the qualities of a strong argument?" Discuss the importance of supporting arguments with reasons and evidence. Tell students that they are going to examine the text to see if the arguments are validated by reasons.

3. Read the first paragraph of the text aloud. Ask, "What is the author's argument?" With a red marker, underline the sentence, "The United States National Park System is a treasure that must be preserved." Have students identify the reasons that support this argument. Model how to underline the reasons with the blue marker on the projected text. Have students do the same on their copies of the text.

4. Place students with partners. Have them reread the rest of the text and continue underlining the argument in red and the reasons or evidence in blue.

5. Distribute copies of the *National Park Claims and Evidence* activity sheet (page 121) to students. Demonstrate how to record the arguments and the supporting reasons.

6. Provide time for students to complete their activity sheets independently.

7. Review students' responses as a class. Encourage students to make corrections as needed.

Writing Connection

1. Tell students that they will have a chance to respond to the text by writing an argument. Explain that they can choose to disagree with the main premise of the argument (national parks need to be preserved) or they can respond to one of the individual arguments in the text.

2. Remind students about the importance of supporting their claims with reasons and evidence. Provide examples of credible and not credible sources and discuss the importance of using credible sources to support arguments.

3. Distribute copies of the *Response Research* activity sheet (page 122) to students. Read the directions aloud. Provide time for students to complete the activity sheet in class or as homework.

4. Distribute copies of the *National Parks Preservation Response* activity sheet (page 123) to students. Provide time for them to write a response to the text. Remind them to include reasons and evidence from credible sources to support their claims.

5. If time permits, have each student switch papers with a partner. Instruct students to read their partner's work and give two compliments and one suggestion for improvement.

Name: _____ **Date:** _____

Objective and Subjective Summaries

Directions: Read the subjective summary below. Rewrite the paragraph to make it objective.

Subjective Summary

The national parks are beautiful places that need to be preserved. Tourists damage national parks by starting wildfires and polluting, but they should not be blamed for everything. Natural occurrences, such as lightning, also start wildfires. Furthermore, many tourists help the national parks by paying entrance fees and donating money to help preserve them. Snowmobiles create noise and scare animals in the national parks. However, it would be very unfair to ban them altogether. Some people enjoy snowmobiling as a form of recreation. The national parks are also in danger because some lands are being sold to private investors and oil drilling in national parks harms the environment. The government needs to do more to protect our national parks.

Objective Summary

_____

_____

_____

_____

_____

_____

_____

_____

_____

_____

_____

_____

_____

Name: _____ **Date:** _____

Language Decoder

Directions: Record examples of figurative language on the chart. Explain the literal and figurative meanings of the phrases.

Sentence from Text	Literal Meaning	Figurative Meaning

How does the use of specific words and figurative language make the author's arguments more effective? Be sure to include examples from the text in your response.

_____

_____

_____

_____

_____

_____

#51505—*Connect to Text: Strategies for Close Reading and Writing* © Shell Education

Name: _____ **Date:** _____

National Park Claims and Evidence

Directions: Record the claims made in the text. Note the evidence provided to support these claims.

Claim	Evidence

Name: _____ **Date:** _____

Response Research

Directions: Write the central argument that will form the basis of your response to the text passage on the lines below. Record the reasons and evidence from your research that can be used to support your central argument. For each reason or piece of evidence, note the source.

Central Argument: _____

_____

Reason #1: _____

_____

_____

Source: _____

Reason #2: _____

_____

_____

Source: _____

Reason #3: _____

_____

_____

Source: _____

Reason #4: _____

_____

_____

Source: _____

Additional reasons: _____

_____

_____

Sources: _____

Name: _____ **Date:** _____

National Parks Preservation Response

Directions: Use the notes from your *Response Research* activity sheet to write your argument on the lines below.

_____

_____

_____

_____

_____

_____

_____

_____

_____

_____

_____

_____

_____

_____

_____

_____

_____

_____

_____

_____

_____

_____

Flag Day Address June 14, 1917

Standards

- Analyze how the author unfolds an analysis or series of ideas or events, including the order in which the points are made, how they are introduced and developed, and the connections that are drawn between them.

- Delineate and evaluate the argument and specific claims in a text, assessing whether the reasoning is valid and the evidence is relevant and sufficient; identify false statements and fallacious reasoning.

- Analyze seminal US documents of historical and literary significance, including how they address related themes and concepts.

- Introduce precise claim(s), distinguish the claim(s) from alternate or opposing claims, and create an organization that establishes clear relationships among claim(s), counterclaims, reasons, and evidence.

Overview

The text in this lesson shows the powerful use of argument text in political debate. In this lesson, students examine the claims, evidence, and themes in President Wilson's speech about the United States' entrance into World War I. They examine the use of the American flag as a symbol and reflect how this use of symbolism supports the objective of the text. They also explore the connections between arguments and reasons and analyze how the text uses historical references to bolster its claims. For the writing connection, students write arguments to express their own opinions on the topic.

Areas of Focus

- main idea
- arguments and claims
- applying and analyzing sources
- claims and counterclaims

Materials

- *Flag Day Address June 14, 1917* (page 125)
- *Introduction Analysis* (page 129)
- *Flag Day Claims and Evidence* (page 130)
- *Historical Analysis* (page 131)
- *Building an Argument* (page 132)
- *War Decisions* (page 133)
- projector or document camera
- colored markers with fine tips
- books and online resources about America's entry into WWI

Flag Day Address June 14, 1917

My Fellow Citizens:

We meet to celebrate Flag Day because this flag which we honor and under which we serve is the emblem of our unity, our power, our thought and purpose as a nation....We celebrate the day of its birth; and from its birth until now it has witnessed a great history, has floated on high the symbol of great events, of a great plan of life worked out by a great people. We are about to carry it into battle, to lift it where it will draw the fire of our enemies. We are about to bid thousands, hundreds of thousands, it may be millions, of our men, the young, the strong, the capable men of the Nation, to go forth and die beneath it on fields of blood far away—for what? For some unaccustomed thing? For something for which it has never sought the fire before? American armies were never before sent across the seas. Why are they sent now? For some new purpose, for which this great flag has never been carried before, or for some old, familiar, heroic purpose for which it has seen men, its own men, die on every battlefield upon which Americans have borne arms since the Revolution? [...]

It is plain enough how we were forced into the war. The extraordinary insults and aggressions of the Imperial German Government left us no self-respecting choice but to take up arms in defense of our rights as a free people and of our honor as a sovereign Government. The military masters of Germany denied us the right to be neutral. They filled our unsuspecting communities with vicious spies and conspirators and sought to corrupt the opinion of our people in their own behalf.

When they found that they could not do that, their agents diligently spread sedition among us and sought to draw our own citizens from their allegiance—and some of those agents were men connected with the official embassy of the German Government itself here in our own capital. They sought by violence to destroy our own industries and arrest our commerce. They tried to incite Mexico to take up arms against us and to draw Japan into a hostile alliance with her—and that, not by indirection but by direct suggestion from the Foreign Office in Berlin. They impudently denied us the use of the seas and repeatedly executed their threat that they would send to their death any of our people who ventured to approach the coasts of Europe. [...]

For us there is but one choice. We have made it. Woe be to the man or group of men that seeks to stand in our way in this day of high resolution when every principle we hold dearest is to be vindicated and made secure for the salvation of the nations. We are ready to plead at the bar of history, and our flag shall wear a new luster. Once more we shall make good with our lives and fortunes the great faith to which we were born, and a new glory shall shine in the face of our people.

Close Reading Activities

First Read (Overview/First Impressions)

1. Distribute copies of the *Flag Day Address June 14, 1917* text (page 125) to students. Have students number each paragraph in the left margin. Encourage them to refer to these numbers as they reference the text throughout the close reading activities.

2. Before reading, remind students that the first read is to help them gather their initial impressions of the text. Remind them to note the following on the text using the suggested marks:

   • questions about the text (?) (write question in the margin)

   • words or phrases they want to learn more about (put box around)

   • words or phrases that seem important (*)

   • areas of interest or confusion (!)

   • related ideas or concepts (⊂⊃) (write connection in the margin)

   • areas of agreement or disagreement (△ = agree ▽ = disagree)

   • questions about credibility or sources (circle)

   • historical connections or questions (draw cloud around)

3. Explain that this text is part of a speech that President Woodrow Wilson gave to the American public on Flag Day—June 14, 1917—as the United States was preparing to enter World War I. Read the text aloud.

4. After the initial reading is complete, provide time for students to revisit their notes and make additional annotations on the text.

5. Use a projector or document camera to display the text. Invite students to discuss their questions, thoughts, and areas of confusion. Encourage students to record these ideas on the text.

Second Read (Main Idea)

1. Display the text using a projector or document camera. Have students reread the first paragraph independently.

2. Ask students to summarize the main points. Record their ideas.

3. Ask students to imagine what it was like to be President Wilson at the time of this speech. Ask, "What challenges did Wilson face?" Discuss the gravity of the decision to enter World War I.

4. Note how the first paragraph of the speech revolves around the American flag. Using a colored marker, underline the words Wilson uses to refer to the flag (unity, power, symbol of great events, etc.).

5. Ask students to discuss the symbolism of the American flag in the speech. As students share their thoughts, take notes and have students take notes in their notebooks.

6. Distribute copies of the *Introduction Analysis* activity sheet (page 129) to students. Have students work independently or in pairs to complete the activity sheet.

7. Review students' answers as a class. Discuss the use of rhetorical questions in the first paragraph to highlight the potential counterpoints and concerns about the decision to enter the war.

Third Read (Arguments and Claims)

1. Have students independently reread the text starting at the second paragraph.

2. Display the text using a projector or document camera. Ask students to identify the main claim in the second paragraph (the US was forced to join the war). Highlight the sentence containing this line on the projected text.

3. Place students with partners. Give each pair a colored marker with a fine tip. Tell them that they will read the rest of the text and number the reasons and evidence that support the main claim.

4. Distribute copies of the *Flag Day Claims and Evidence* activity sheet (page 130) to students. Provide time for students to work together to complete the activity sheet.

5. Review students' responses as a class.

6. Direct students' attention to the last paragraph in the text. Have students underline the main claim, number the reasons, and record them on the activity sheet.

7. Discuss students' responses. Then, tell students that the next paragraph, which is not included in the passage, explains that the "military masters of Germany" are responsible for the war.

Fourth Read (Applying and Analyzing Sources)

1. Ask students to consider the role of argument texts in politics and history. Discuss how politicians frequently use argument texts to communicate their agendas and convince the public to support their ideas. Have the class brainstorm specific examples of the use of argument texts in politics (inaugural addresses, campaign speeches, etc.).

2. Ask students to think about the historic events that influenced Wilson's speech. Have them reread the text and take notes about the historical influences at work. Discuss their ideas as a class.

3. Distribute copies of the *Historical Analysis* activity sheet (page 131) to students. Provide time for the students to complete the activity sheet independently.

4. Review students' answers as a class. Discuss how Wilson links the political events of the time (Germany's military aggression) to American history.

Writing Connection

1. On the board, write the question, "Should the United States have entered World War I?" Tell them that they will conduct research to write an argument in response to that question.

2. Remind students about the importance of supporting claims with reasons and evidence. Explain that they should give at least three reasons to support each of their claims, two opposing or alternate claims, and two counterarguments to the opposing claims.

3. Distribute copies of the *Building an Argument* activity sheet (page 132) to students. Using a projector or document camera, display the activity sheet. Read the directions aloud.

4. Think aloud as you give an example of a claim (e.g., The United States should have entered World War I), an opposing argument (e.g., Many American lives were lost as a result of entering the war), and a counterclaim (e.g., Many *more* American lives would have been lost if the Central Powers conquered Europe and decided to invade North America).

5. Have students research America's entry into World War I. Provide time for them to complete the outline on their activity sheets.

6. Distribute copies of the *War Decisions* activity sheet (page 133) to students. Have students use their outlines to write arguments.

7. Ask students to read their arguments in small groups.

Name: _____   **Date:** _____

Introduction Analysis

Directions: Answer the questions below using specific details and evidence from the text.

1. Why did Wilson choose to introduce his speech with a discussion of the American flag? What symbolic role does the flag play in the first paragraph of the speech?

_____

_____

_____

_____

_____

_____

_____

_____

_____

2. What is the purpose of the questions in the first paragraph?

_____

_____

_____

_____

_____

_____

_____

Name: _____   **Date:** _____

Flag Day Claims and Evidence

Directions: Record the claims and supporting reasons or evidence in the text passage. Be sure to refer to the text passage in your responses.

1. Claim: _____

_____

Reasons or evidence: _____

_____

_____

_____

2. Claim: _____

_____

Reasons or evidence: _____

_____

_____

_____

3. Claim: _____

_____

Reasons or evidence: _____

_____

_____

_____

 #51505—Connect to Text: Strategies for Close Reading and Writing

Name: _____   **Date:** _____

Historical Analysis

Directions: Answer the questions using information from the text to support your ideas.

1. What was the objective of Wilson's speech? How do you know?

_____

_____

2. How would Wilson answer his last question in the first paragraph?

> American armies were never before sent across the seas. Why are they sent now? For some new purpose, for which this great flag has never been carried before, or for some old, familiar, heroic purpose for which it has seen men, its own men, die on every battlefield upon which Americans have borne arms since the Revolution?

_____

_____

_____

_____

3. How does Wilson's last question above relate to American history?

_____

_____

_____

_____

4. Why does Wilson blame the "military masters of Germany," rather than the entire country of Germany, for forcing the US to enter the war? How does this tactic help him accomplish the objective of his speech?

_____

_____

_____

_____

Name: _____ **Date:** _____

Building an Argument

Directions: Research America's entry into World War I. Take a stance on what you think America should have done and complete the outline below.

Should the United States Have Entered World War I?

Claim: _____

_____

_____

Reason #1: _____

_____

Reason #2: _____

_____

Reason #3: _____

_____

Opposing Argument: _____

_____

Counterargument: _____

_____

Conclusion: _____

_____

#51505—Connect to Text: Strategies for Close Reading and Writing © Shell Education

Name: _____   **Date:** _____

War Decisions

Directions: Use the notes from your *Building an Argument* activity sheet to write your argument on the lines below.

Should the United States Have Entered World War I?

_____

_____

_____

_____

_____

_____

_____

_____

_____

_____

_____

_____

_____

_____

_____

_____

_____

_____

_____

_____

_____

_____

_____

#51505—Connect to Text: Strategies for Close Reading and Writing   © Shell Education

Connect to Literature

Literature has always played an important role in reading and writing instruction. Literature serves the double purpose of entertainment and education. Stories draw the reader in with their enticing storylines and creative characters while conveying important themes, morals, and information about a wide variety of topics.

What Is Literature?

While the general definition of the term "literature" can refer to any type of written text, it is most often used to describe a category of text, including story, drama, and poetry. According to Sisson and Sisson (2014), "Literature refers to stories that are invented through the imagination of the mind with different literary genres sharing some similar characteristics, such as adhering to a universal narrative text structure" (50). Each of the three distinct types of literature (story, drama, and poetry) includes several different literary genres. Stories include folktales, legends, fables, realistic fiction, myths, fantasy, and adventure stories. The category of drama includes plays in both written and filmed formats. Poetry comes in many forms, including limericks, haiku, narrative poems, sonnets, odes, ballads, and epics.

Literature and Today's Standards

The Common Core State Standards for Reading Literature define the skills and knowledge that students must demonstrate when reading stories, dramas, and poetry. These include critical-thinking skills and the ability to analyze complex literary texts. Like the CCSS for informational texts, the literature standards are divided into three categories: key ideas and details, craft and structure, and integration of knowledge and ideas. Close reading activities help students connect to literary texts and practice the skills in all three categories.

Close Reading and Literature

Key Ideas and Details

Close reading activities for key ideas and details help students examine how the details of a text support the development of the story. Students in younger grades learn how to identify key details, such as *who, what, where, when, why,* and *how,* by asking and answering questions. Older students analyze texts for explicit details, inferred details, and areas of uncertainty.

Students also learn how to summarize and retell stories by highlighting important words and phrases and using the words to summarize the text. Furthermore, close reading can be used to help students study various literary elements, such as setting, characters, and important events. For example, a close study of the words used to describe the setting in *The Legend of Sleepy Hollow* reveals how the author sets the tone for the story.

Craft and Structure

Close reading activities to analyze craft and structure are designed to show students how word choice, text structure, and author's point of view and purpose impact texts. Students examine text structure at various levels, beginning with word analysis. They learn to identify figurative language and to explain its effect on texts. Close reading activities also guide students in examining how specific words or phrases contribute to the tone.

In addition to studying the effects of certain words and phrases, students use close reading to examine text structure. They learn how readers can use the structure of a text to help them better understand its content. Students also make connections between sentences, paragraphs, and stanzas to see how they relate to each other and to the work as a whole.

Lastly, close reading and text-dependent questions help students explore the author's point of view and purpose. Students learn to distinguish the author's point of view from their own points of view and to determine how characters' points of view affect narratives. In addition, they learn how the author's purpose for writing shapes the style of a text.

Integration of Knowledge and Ideas

The third category of standards requires students to integrate and evaluate ideas presented in different versions of the same narrative. Students must use their knowledge about central ideas, themes, characters, word choice, text structure, etc., to compare multiple texts, as well as narratives presented in different formats. For instance, in the elementary grades, students examine the details presented in the text and compare this to details presented in the accompanying illustrations. Older students compare the same text in different formats, such as the play version and the film version of a text. Close reading activities can also be used to compare multiple versions of the same text, such as various retellings of the story *Little Red Riding Hood*. Although the skills required by these standards are challenging and complex, close reading provides the necessary scaffolding for students to learn how to complete these types of comparisons accurately and independently.

Writing Literature

In addition to helping students comprehend texts on deeper levels, close reading also helps students improve their own narrative writing skills. Close reading requires students to study the literary techniques that professional authors use. Students can then apply those techniques to their own writing. For example, after studying the theme of perseverance in the fable, *Why the Chipmunk Has Black Stripes*, students can practice writing personal narratives with the same theme.

Mentor texts also help students apply knowledge about text structure to their own writing. By studying the structures of various types of texts, students learn how structure affects the meaning, tone, and overall message of literature. For instance, after studying a text told from a first-person omniscient point of view, students are better equipped to use this point of view effectively in their own writing. Close reading activities also help students apply other literary techniques, such as figurative language, to enhance their own writing. Overall, close reading is not only an effective technique for increasing reading comprehension, but also a useful tool for helping students apply literary techniques to their own writing.

Text-Dependent Questions and Prompts to Support Close Reading and Writing of Literature

The following text-dependent questions and prompts cover some of the broad areas of focus in literacy. When planning close reading and writing activities, these questions and prompts should be tailored to fit the selected text passages.

Key Ideas and Details

- What does the author explicitly tell you about the setting/characters/ events in the story? What can you infer? Support your answer with textual evidence.

- What happens in the story? What are the important details? Remember to include specific examples from the text in your answer.

- What lesson does the author want the reader to learn from the story? How does the author communicate this lesson? Use details from the text to support your answer.

- How does the author develop the theme of the story through the plot/ character/setting/dialogue? Include specific examples from the text to support your answer.

- Describe some of the key details about the characters/setting/events in the story. How do these details effect your overall understanding of the characters/setting/events?

Craft and Structure

- What is the tone of the text? What language does the author use to create this tone? Be sure to cite specific examples from the text.

- What is the role of figurative language or imagery in the text? Be sure to support your answer with specific examples from the text.

- What is the sequence of events in the story? Why is this sequence important to the overall effect of the story?

- How do all of the text's individual parts (chapters, stanzas, scenes, etc.) come together to create a cohesive text? Be sure to refer to the text in your answer.

- What role does point of view play in the development of the story? Provide examples from the text in your answer.

- Describe the different points of view of each character in the story. How do these points of view affect the development of the theme(s) in the text? Be sure to use specific words and phrases from the text to support your answer.

Integration of Knowledge and Ideas

- How do the illustrations and text work together to create a meaningful experience for the reader?

- What details can you learn from the text? What details can you learn from the illustrations?

- What do the illustrations tell us about the mood/characters/settings/events/themes of the story?

- How is this version of the story different from that version of the same story? How are the two versions similar?

- How are the characters/settings/events/themes similar and different between the two versions of the same story?

- How does the audio/filmed/live version of the text differ from the written version of the text? How are the two versions the same?

- What themes are present in both texts? Provide examples from each text to support your answer.

At the Beach

Overview

Poetry presents numerous options for close reading activities. In this lesson, the first and second close reading activities focus on familiarizing students with the poem and identifying key details. The next close reading activity helps students think about the ways in which poetry is different from other types of literature. The final activity asks students to analyze the connections between the text and the illustration. For the writing connection, students write their own narrative about a personal experience. Overall, this lesson provides students with an in-depth introduction to the unique characteristics and distinguishing traits of poetry while also giving them an opportunity to express themselves in writing.

Areas of Focus

- key details
- text structure
- visual media
- narrating events

Materials

- *At the Beach* (page 140)
- *Beach Question* (page 144)
- *Rhyming Word Pairs* (page 145)
- *Beach Picture* (page 146)
- *My Favorite Place* (page 147)
- chart paper
- projector or document camera
- coloring supplies

Standards

- With prompting and support, ask and answer questions about key details in a text.
- Recognize common types of texts.
- With prompting and support, describe the relationship between illustrations and the story in which they appear.
- Use a combination of drawing, dictating, and writing to narrate a single event or several loosely linked events, tell about the events in the order in which they occurred, and provide a reaction to what happened.

At the Beach

The waves crash upon the sand,
The sun is shining bright.
The sand is warm beneath my toes,
My brother flies a kite.

The birds cry up in the sky,
The kids are all at play.
I want to run and jump and sing,
I hope we stay all day!

#51505—Connect to Text: Strategies for Close Reading and Writing

Close Reading Activities

First Read (Overview/First Impressions)

1. Rewrite the poem *At the Beach* (page 140) on chart paper and display it for the class.

2. Tell students that you are going to read a poem aloud to them. Ask them to listen carefully for new or interesting words.

3. Read the poem aloud, using your finger or a pointer to help students track the text.

4. Ask students to share their initial impressions and questions about the poem. Record students' ideas on chart paper.

Second Read (Key Details)

1. Read the poem aloud again line by line. Have students read along with you. Number the lines of the poem.

2. Read the first line again. Say, "There are two words in this line that I think really capture what this sentence is about. These are key words." Underline the key words *waves* and *sand*. Explain that without these key words, we wouldn't get a very clear picture in our minds.

3. Repeat Step 2 for the other lines of the poem.

4. On chart paper, list the underlined words. Read the list aloud to the class. Tell students that these words are the key words that capture what the poem is really about.

5. Distribute copies of the *Beach Question* activity sheet (page 144) to students. Say, "Sometimes after we read a poem or story, we are still wondering about it. We have some questions that the author did not answer. For example, I wonder if the boy or girl telling the story got to go swimming in the water."

6. Think aloud as you model how to ask a question using one of the key words from the key word list. (*Was it a hot day? Did the narrator get to fly a kite, too?*)

7. Provide time for the students to complete the *Beach Question* activity sheet. If necessary, have students dictate their questions and record them on their activity sheets.

8. If time permits, allow several students to come to the front of the class to share their questions with the class.

Third Read (Text Structure)

1. Display the poem using a projector or document camera. Ask, "Can you tell just by looking at the text that this is a poem? How can you tell?" Discuss how the structure of poems is often different from other types of text.

2. Have students close their eyes and listen closely as you read the poem aloud to the class. Ask them what they notice about how the poem sounds.

3. Write the words *bright, kite, day*, and *play* on chart paper. Read the rhyming pairs aloud. Explain that these words rhyme because they share the same ending sounds. Tell the class that many, but not all, poems include words that rhyme.

4. Distribute copies of the *Rhyming Word Pairs* activity sheet (page 145) to students. Display a copy of the activity sheet using a projector or document camera. Read the instructions aloud. Have students follow along as you read the words on the left side of the paper aloud.

5. Demonstrate how to complete the first item on the activity sheet by drawing a line between the words *dog* and *log*. Ask students to say other words that also rhyme with *dog*.

6. Give students time to complete the rest of the activity sheet independently.

7. When everyone is finished, invite students to share their rhyming word pairs and make corrections, as needed.

Fourth Read (Visual Media)

1. Have students examine the illustration. Ask, "What does the picture show?" Discuss the illustration in detail.

2. Have students read the poem aloud chorally.

3. Ask, "What specific parts of the poem does the picture show?" As students respond, refer back to the text and point to the words that relate to the picture.

4. Give each student a *Beach Picture* activity sheet (page 146). Read the directions aloud. Explain that students must show at least one specific detail from the poem.

5. Provide time for students to complete their illustrations. As they work, circulate and ask each student to tell you which parts of the poem they are showing in their drawings.

6. If time permits, allow volunteers to share their work with the rest of the class. Have each volunteer explain the part of the poem shown in his or her drawing.

#51505—Connect to Text: Strategies for Close Reading and Writing   © Shell Education

Writing Connection

1. Distribute copies of *At the Beach* (page 140) to students. Have them read the poem with partners. Ask them to tell their reading partner what the poem is about.

2. Review the aspects of narrative text covered in the close reading activities (key details, types of text, and visual media). Say, "*At the Beach* is a poem about a place the author likes to go—the beach. Now, it is your turn to write about a place you like to go."

3. Ask students to share their topic ideas. Record their ideas on chart paper.

4. Use a projector or document camera to display a copy of the *My Favorite Place* activity sheet (page 147). Think aloud as you model how to choose a place to write about and draw a picture of the place. Continue to think aloud as you write several sentences about the place. Include sensory details about what you saw, felt, and heard.

5. Give each student a copy of the *My Favorite Place* activity sheet. Provide time for them to draw their pictures and write or dictate about their experiences.

6. When everyone is finished, encourage students to share their work with the rest of the class. If possible, display their work on a classroom bulletin board or bind the pages into a class book.

Name: _____ **Date:** _____

Beach Question

Directions: Write a question about the poem below.

At the Beach

The waves crash upon the sand,
The sun is shining bright.
The sand is warm beneath my toes,
My brother flies a kite.

The birds cry up in the sky,
The kids are all at play.
I want to run and jump and sing,
I hope we stay all day!

My Question:

_____

_ _

_____

_ _

_____

#51505—Connect to Text: Strategies for Close Reading and Writing © Shell Education

Name: _____ **Date:** _____

Rhyming Word Pairs

Directions: Draw a line between each pair of rhyming words.

dog

bun

hat

jet

pig

cat

sun

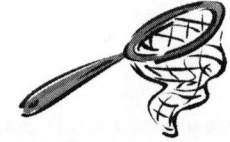

log

net

wig

#51505—Connect to Text: Strategies for Close Reading and Writing

Name: _____ **Date:** _____

Beach Picture

Directions: Draw a picture to go with the poem, *At the Beach.* Add at least one specific detail from the poem.

#51505—Connect to Text: Strategies for Close Reading and Writing

Name: _____ **Date:** _____

My Favorite Place

Directions: Draw a picture of your favorite place. Write about what you see, hear, and do there.

_____

- -

_____

_____

- -

_____

_____

- -

_____

Why the Chipmunk Has Black Stripes

Overview

This close reading lesson explores the rich genre of fables and folktales from other cultures. As students read and examine the Iroquois folktale *Why the Chipmunk Has Black Stripes,* they practice retelling and identifying the central message, or moral, of the story. In addition, they analyze the main characters in order to see how the words used to describe them relate to both the events and the moral of the story. In the last close reading activity, students read the story as a group, with each student reading the part of a different character. Then, students examine the characters' points of view and reflect on how the reading experience allowed them to better understand these viewpoints. In the final portion of the lesson, students write a narrative about the theme of the fable: perseverance.

Standards

- Recount stories, including fables and folktales from diverse cultures, and determine their central message, lesson, or moral.
- Describe how characters in a story respond to major events and challenges.
- Acknowledge differences in the points of view of characters, including by speaking in a different voice for each character when reading dialogue aloud.
- Write narratives in which they recount a well-elaborated event or short sequence of events, include details to describe actions, thoughts, and feelings, use temporal words to signal event order, and provide a sense of closure.

Areas of Focus

- summarizing
- characters
- point of view
- describing actions

Materials

- *Why the Chipmunk Has Black Stripes* (page 149)
- *Story Summary* (page 153)
- *Character Analysis* (page 154)
- *Character Point of View* (page 155)
- *Perseverance Story Planner* (page 156)
- *I Can Persevere* (page 157)
- projector or document camera
- chart paper
- two different colored markers or crayons (per student)
- highlighters

Why the Chipmunk Has Black Stripes

"Friends," said the porcupine, "we have met here to settle a great question: Shall we have night all the time, or day?" At this, all the animals began to talk at once. The night animals kept shouting, "Night, night! Always night!" Others of the animals cried, "Day, day! Always day!" Still others called for "Day and night!" There was so much noise that it could not be decided what was best.

At last the animals grew tired of calling and the shouting ceased. Of the night animals, the voice of the bear alone was heard. He had a big voice and still kept calling, "Night, night! Always night!"

Then the bear, too, became tired. He thought he would take a short nap, but all night long the wide-awake chipmunk kept up his song. Out of the dark came his voice, sure and cheery, "We will have light—and then night. We will have light—and then night! Chee, chee, chee!" Before the animals knew it, the sun began to rise.

At the first rays of light, the bear sat up, blinked, and rubbed his eyes. He saw that while he had slept, light had indeed come. The bear was very angry. He struck at the chipmunk with his paw. But he was clumsy, and the chipmunk was spry! The chipmunk laughed and sprang into a hole of a hollow tree nearby. But those black stripes on the chipmunk's back show where the paw of the black bear touched him as he slipped into the tree.

Ever since this council, and the little chipmunk called so long and loud for "light and night," we have had day and night.

Close Reading Activities

First Read (Overview/First Impressions)

1. Distribute copies of *Why the Chipmunk Has Black Stripes* (page 149) to students. Tell students that this text is a story that comes from the Iroquois tribe, a group of American Indians in the Northeastern United States.

2. Use a projector or document camera to display the text. Demonstrate how to number each line on the left side of the text. Have students number their copies. Explain that they should refer to these numbers when quoting from the text.

3. Before reading the passage, remind students that the first read is to help them gather their initial impressions of the text. Ask them to note any of the following topics directly on the text during the reading using the suggested marks:

   - questions about the text (?) (write question in the margin)

   - words or phrases they want to learn more about (put box around)

   - words or phrases that seem important (*)

   - areas of interest or confusion (!)

4. Read the text aloud to the class.

5. Provide time for the students to revisit their notes and make additional annotations on the text.

6. Use a projector or document camera to display the text. Have students share their questions, thoughts, and areas of confusion. Demonstrate how to record these on the text.

Second Read (Summarizing)

1. Distribute copies of *Why the Chipmunk Has Black Stripes* to students. Have them read the text independently.

2. Tell students that they will retell the story of the chipmunk and his stripes. Explain that their retelling will be in their own words, but it must include the story's main idea and key details.

3. Place students in five groups and assign each group one paragraph of the text. Distribute copies of the *Story Summary* activity sheet (page 153) to students. Read the directions aloud.

4. After students have written their summaries, ask one representative from each group to read the summary aloud. Record the summaries and display them using a projector or document camera.

5. Have each group work together to retell the fable from beginning to end.

6. Ask students to reread the fourth paragraph of text. Ask, "What is the moral, or lesson, of this story?" Remind students to support their answers with evidence from the text.

7. Discuss the story's message of perseverance. Have students write a sentence summarizing the moral of the story at the bottom of their *Story Summary* activity sheets.

8. Provide time for students to read their sentences to partners.

Third Read (Characters)

1. Tell students that this activity will focus on the story's characters. Ask students to name the characters as you list them on chart paper.

2. Use a projector or document camera to display the story. Model for students how to code the story with two different colors—one color for words that describe the chipmunk and one color for words that describe the bear.

3. Give each student two different colored markers or crayons. Have them code the text.

4. Divide students into pairs. Distribute copies of the *Character Analysis* activity sheet (page 154) to students. Have pairs work together to complete the activity sheet.

5. After everyone has finished, discuss students' responses as a class. Remind students to refer back to the text when explaining their answers.

Fourth Read (Point of View)

1. Place students in groups of four and assign each student a number 1–4. Explain that everyone with the number one will read the part of narrator, number two will read the porcupine's dialogue, number three will read the bear's dialogue, and number four will read the chipmunk's dialogue. Help students highlight their lines in the story.

2. Have students read the story aloud in their groups, with each student reading the assigned role. Encourage students to use a unique but understandable voice for their character.

3. Distribute copies of the *Character Point of View* activity sheet (page 155) to students. Have students work together in their groups to complete the activity sheet.

4. As a class, discuss the benefits of using different voices to represent the characters in the story. Ask, "How did the experience of having different students read each character help you understand the characters' points of view?" Remind students to cite evidence from the text in their answers.

Writing Connection

1. Review the aspects of narrative text covered in the close reading activities (central lesson, characters, point of view). Remind students about the story's central message of perseverance.

2. Tell students that they will have a chance to write their own story about a time that they had to persevere. Provide an example from a time in your own life where you had to persevere.

3. Conduct a whole-class brainstorming session. Record students' ideas on chart paper.

4. Distribute copies of the *Perseverance Story Planner* activity sheet (page 156) to students. Display the activity sheet using a projector or document camera. Think aloud as you complete an example.

5. Provide time for students to complete their own *Perseverance Story Planner* activity sheets.

6. Distribute copies of the *I Can Persevere* activity sheet (page 157) to students. Model for students how to use the ideas from the story planner to write a personal narrative. Demonstrate how to elaborate on the basic outline by describing your actions, thoughts, and feelings about the events.

7. Provide students time to write their personal narratives.

8. If possible, display the finished stories on a classroom or hallway bulletin board or bind them into a class book.

Name: _____ **Date:** _____

Story Summary

Directions: Complete the chart below. Write key words from your assigned paragraph. Then, write a short summary of the paragraph.

> **Paragraph #:**

> **Key Words:**

> **Summary:**

What is the main idea, or moral, of this story? How do you know?

_____

_____

_____

_____

_____

Name: _____ Date: _____

Character Analysis

Directions: Record the words that describe the chipmunk and the bear in the boxes below. Then, answer the questions using evidence from the text.

Bear	Chipmunk

1. How are the bear and the chipmunk alike?

_____

_____

2. How are the bear and the chipmunk different?

_____

_____

3. What qualities help the chipmunk win the argument?

_____

_____

Name: _____ **Date:** _____

Character Point of View

Directions: Describe each character's point of view. Answer the *How do I know?* question with evidence from the text.

Bear's point of view:

How do I know?

Chipmunk's point of view:

How do I know?

Name: _____ **Date:** _____

Perseverance Story Planner

Directions: Complete each section below.

1. Tell what happened in order:

> First,

> Next,

> Last,

2. Write a conclusion that tells what you learned and how you felt about it.

_____

_____

_____

  #51505—Connect to Text: Strategies for Close Reading and Writing

Name: _____ **Date:** _____

I Can Persevere

Directions: Write a personal narrative about a time you persevered. Use your notes from the *Perseverance Story Planner* as a guide. Tell about how you acted, thought, and felt.

_____

_____

_____

_____

_____

_____

_____

_____

_____

_____

_____

_____

Captain Butterbeard Addresses His Crew

Standards

- Quote accurately from a text when explaining what the text says explicitly and when drawing inferences from the text.

- Determine the meaning of words and phrases as they are used in a text, including figurative language such as metaphors and similes.

- Describe how a narrator's or speaker's point of view influences how events are described.

- Use narrative techniques, such as dialogue, description, and pacing, to develop experiences and events or show the responses of characters to situations.

Overview

In this lesson, students analyze the effects of word choice and point of view on a text. With the first reading of the text, students gather their initial impressions and ask questions for clarification. The second close reading activity guides students through the process of putting together evidence from the text with their own ideas to make inferences about details that are not stated explicitly. In the third activity, students identify figurative language in the text and examine how nonliteral descriptions convey thoughts, feelings, and emotions. The final close reading activity focuses on point of view. Students determine the text's point of view (third person) and analyze how it affects the way the author describes the main character's feelings. In the writing connection, students rewrite the first paragraph of the text using figurative language and a different point of view.

Areas of Focus

- inferences

- figurative language

- point of view

- expressive writing

Materials

- *Captain Butterbeard Addresses His Crew* (page 159)

- *Pirate Inferences* (page 164)

- *Figurative Language* (page 165)

- *Do Pirates Have Feelings?* (page 166)

- *I Address My Crew* (page 167)

- projector or document camera

Captain Butterbeard Addresses His Crew

Captain Butterbeard looked suspiciously at his crew. Which one of them would betray him? He had selected each one of them. His ship had the foulest, most cutthroat crew of any pirate vessel in the Caribbean. While that made them very good at their jobs, it meant that not one of them could be trusted. The crew operated like a pack of wolves. The strongest one would lead until he was challenged successfully by an underling. Captain Butterbeard liked that about them.

"Ye scurvy sea dogs," Captain Butterbeard sneered. "Listen up! This here island is Tortuga and that there ship is the *Bonny Main*. Tonight, she plans to sail out of port laden with jewels, gold, and riches of all kinds. By tomorrow morning, her cargo will be stowed in our hold, and her crew will be secured in our brig, ready to ransom!"

The captain strutted confidently in front of the assembled crew. He knew that his biggest threat was not from the defenders on the *Bonny Main*. No, the risk was this crew would turn on him if they thought he showed even the slightest weakness. He must always project strength.

"I don't have to tell ye mates that we stand to make a small fortune on this haul, but we have to work together!" The captain stopped suddenly and stared directly into the eyes of a particularly cruel-looking crewman. "Every man here will pull his own weight, or he will be spending time in Davy Jones's locker!" The man shifted uncomfortably and looked away.

"Are ye with me, lads?" the captain finished.

The crew cheered enthusiastically, and then rushed off to follow his orders. Captain Butterbeard allowed himself a cautious smile. There would be no mutiny today!

Close Reading Activities

First Read (Overview/First Impressions)

1. Distribute copies of *Captain Butterbeard Addresses His Crew* (page 159) to students.

2. Use a projector or document camera to display the text. Demonstrate how to number each line of the passage on the left side of the text. Have students number their copies. Explain that they should refer to these numbers when quoting from the text.

3. Before reading the passage, remind students that the first read is to help them gather their initial impressions of the text. Ask them to note any of the following topics directly on the text during the reading using the suggested marks:

   - questions about the text (?) (write question in the margin)

   - words or phrases they want to learn more about (put box around)

   - words or phrases that seem important (*)

   - areas of interest or confusion (!)

   - related ideas or concepts (⟳) (write connection in the margin)

4. Have students read the text independently.

5. When students finish reading, ask them to revisit their notes and make additional annotations on the text.

6. Use a projector or document camera to display the text. Have students share their questions, thoughts, and areas of confusion. Demonstrate how to record these on the text.

Second Read (Inferences)

1. Remind students that an inference is a conclusion that readers make by putting together evidence from the text with their own ideas and background knowledge. Give the following example: "If I tell you that Eduardo didn't sleep well last night, and he is having trouble concentrating, what inference can you make?" Discuss how it is reasonable to infer that Eduardo is tired.

2. Tell students that they will use clues from the text plus their own ideas to make inferences. Explain that these inferences will help them understand the story on a deeper level. Display *Captain Butterbeard Addresses His Crew* using a projector or document camera. Read the second paragraph of the text aloud as students follow along.

3. Ask, "What inferences can you make from this paragraph?" Draw a T-chart on the board. Label one column *Text Says...*and the other column *I Know....* Have students differentiate between the details stated explicitly in the text and the background knowledge that they used to infer that the pirates plan to board the *Bonny Main*, take the cargo, and capture the crew. If students need more scaffolding, reread the two sentences starting with, "Tonight, she plans to sail...." Ask, "What do you think Butterbeard plans to do between 'tonight' and 'tomorrow morning'? Why do you think that?" (*Because the text says "tomorrow morning, her cargo will be stowed in our hold, and her crew will be secured in our brig, ready to ransom!" I know from watching movies about pirates that pirates ambush other ships and steal their cargo and kidnap their crew members.*)

4. Distribute copies of the *Pirate Inferences* activity sheet (page 164) to students. Read the directions aloud.

5. Divide students into pairs. Provide time for pairs to complete the activity sheet.

6. When students have completed the activity sheets, discuss the answers as a whole class. Add their answers to the Text Says.../I Know... T-chart on the board. This will ensure that students cite evidence from the text.

Third Read (Figurative Language)

1. Write the following sentences on the board:

   • *He moved like a turtle.*

   • *His desk is a disaster area.*

   • *The classroom was as hot as an oven.*

   • *The burglar was a sly fox.*

2. Tell students that these are examples of figurative language. Explain that figurative language is the use of words and phrases to mean something other than what the words literally say. It is a tool that authors use to help readers visualize more clearly.

3. Write the words *simile* and *metaphor* on the board. Explain that these are two types of figurative language. Tell students that a simile is a comparison that uses the words *like* or *as*. Have students point out the two similes on the board. Write an *S* next to the first and third sample sentences.

4. Explain that a metaphor is a stronger comparison that does not use the words *like* or *as*. Write an M next to the second and fourth sample sentences.

5. Have students reread the first paragraph of the text, *Captain Butterbeard Addresses His Crew*. Ask them to underline examples of figurative language.

6. Display the text using a projector or document camera. Ask a volunteer to come up and underline the figurative language in the paragraph. Discuss the meaning of the sentence, "The crew was like a pack of wolves." Have students identify the type of figurative language (simile) and the sentence that describes its meaning ("The strongest one would lead until he was challenged successfully by an underling."). Discuss how this simile contributes to the reader's understanding of Captain Butterbeard's feelings.

7. Distribute copies of the *Figurative Language* activity sheet (page 165) to students. Place students in small groups of 3 to 4 students. Have the students work together to complete the activity sheet.

8. Allow time for students to share their responses with the class.

Fourth Read (Point of View)

1. Review the concept of point of view. Ask, "Who is telling the story in *Captain Butterbeard Addresses His Crew*?" Help the class identify the point of view in the text passage (*third-person point of view*).

2. Select a student volunteer to reread the first paragraph of the text aloud to the class. After listening to the paragraph, have students turn to a partner and summarize the paragraph using their own words.

3. Discuss how the first paragraph explains Captain Butterbeard's feelings about the plan to take over the *Bonny Main*. Ask the class to identify his feelings (nervous, suspicious, proud, etc.) and write them on the board.

4. Distribute copies of the *Do Pirates Have Feelings?* activity sheet (page 166) to students. Read the directions aloud.

5. Using a projector or document camera, demonstrate how to write the listed feelings from Step 3 in the left column of the chart. Think aloud as you model how to choose evidence from the text that proves one of the feelings. Copy the phrase or sentence in the right column of the chart.

6. Provide time for the students to complete the activity sheet independently.

7. Allow time for students to share their responses with the class. Record the text evidence on a projected copy of the activity sheet.

Writing Connection

1. Review the emotions expressed by Captain Butterbeard in the first paragraph of the text. Discuss the difference between expressing feelings and emotions in the first person point of view and the third-person point of view.

2. Write the first sentence from the text on the board and read it aloud to the class. Have the class identify the primary feeling expressed in this sentence (*suspicion*). Ask the class to suggest ways to express this feeling using the first person point of view. Record their responses on the board. For example, "My shoulders felt tense and my thoughts swirled as I suspiciously eyed my crew."

3. Tell students that they are going to rewrite the first paragraph of the text using the first person point of view. Explain that this is not just an exercise in replacing *Captain Butterbeard/he/him/etc.*, for *I/me/my/etc.* Instead, students must think about what the captain would say and how he would say it if he were describing his own situation. Ask students to use at least one simile or metaphor in the paragraph.

4. Distribute copies of the *I Address My Crew* activity sheet (page 167) to students. Read the directions aloud. Provide time for students to complete the writing activity independently.

5. Place students with partners and have them read their paragraphs aloud to each other. Require students to give one general compliment and one suggestion to improve their partners' use of first person point of view.

6. Provide time for students to make revisions to their work.

7. Invite volunteers to read their paragraphs aloud to the class. Discuss how point of view affects the way authors express feelings and events in their writing.

8. If possible, display the finished stories on a bulletin board.

Name: _____ Date: _____

Pirate Inferences

Directions: Complete the chart using evidence from the text and your own ideas to make inferences.

Question: How does Captain Butterbeard feel about the "cruel-looking crewman"?

Text Says...	Inference	I Know...

Question: Was Captain Butterbeard pleased with the crew's reaction to his plan?

Text Says...	Inference	I Know...

Name: _____ **Date:** _____

Figurative Language

Directions: Read each sentence. Underline the two words being compared. Identify the type of figurative language by circling either *simile* or *metaphor*. On the lines below each sentence, explain the meaning of the figurative language.

1. The acrobat soared like a bird through the air. (simile) (metaphor)

_____

_____

2. He ate his food like a vacuum cleaner. (simile) (metaphor)

_____

_____

3. You are my sunshine. (simile) (metaphor)

_____

_____

4. She ran as fast as a cheetah. (simile) (metaphor)

_____

_____

5. Before the show, his legs were rubber. (simile) (metaphor)

_____

_____

#51505—*Connect to Text: Strategies for Close Reading and Writing* **165**

Name: _____ **Date:** _____

Do Pirates Have Feelings?

Directions: In the left column of the chart, list the feelings that Captain Butterbeard felt. Find a phrase or sentence in the text that gives evidence for each feeling.

Feeling	Text Evidence

#51505—Connect to Text: Strategies for Close Reading and Writing © Shell Education

Name: _____ **Date:** _____

I Address My Crew

Directions: Rewrite the first paragraph of the text using the first person point of view. Use at least one metaphor or simile in your writing.

_____

_____

_____

_____

_____

_____

_____

_____

_____

_____

_____

_____

_____

_____

_____

A Midsummer Night's Dream

Standards

- Determine the meaning of words and phrases as they are used in a text, including figurative and connotative meanings; analyze the impact of a specific word choice on meaning and tone.

- Analyze how a particular sentence, chapter, scene, or stanza fits into the overall structure of a text and contributes to the development of the theme, setting, or plot.

- Compare and contrast the experience of reading a story, drama, or poem to listening to or viewing an audio, video, or live version of the text, including contrasting what they "see" and "hear" when reading the text to what they perceive when they listen or watch.

- Use narrative techniques, such as dialogue, pacing, and description, to develop experiences, events, and/or characters.

Overview

Dramas are distinct from other types of literature in several ways. First, dramas rely on dialogue to convey key details about characters, plot, theme, and tone. Secondly, dramas are written for performance, so they often include sections of text that serve a functional, rather than narrative, purpose. For example, dramas often include stage directions for actors, instructions for set changes, and information about the actors' costumes and props. In this lesson, students read a scene from a Shakespearean play. They analyze the effects of figurative language and specific sentences on the overall text. Students also compare and contrast the written drama with a filmed performance of the play. In the writing connection activity, students apply what they have learned to write dialogue that extends the scene.

Areas of Focus

- figurative language

- connecting information

- applying and analyzing sources

- writing dialogue

Materials

- *A Midsummer Night's Dream Act II, Scene I* (page 169)

- *Creating Comparisons* (page 173)

- *Text Connections* (page 174)

- *Similarities and Differences* (page 175)

- *Shakespeare Reinvented* (page 176)

- projector or document camera

- index cards

- video clip of Act II, Scene I

- video recorder (*optional*)

A Midsummer Night's Dream

Act II, Scene I

Excerpt from William Shakespeare

Titania: This child that you wish to take from me is not my own but belongs to a wonderful friend of mine. During her pregnancy, we used to sit together on the yellow sands of the beach on cool evenings, smelling the salty air. Together we would watch as the ships came into the harbor, heavy with their treasures, and she would compare her rounded pregnant belly with the ships' full sails. Laughing, she would talk about how the sails would billow out curved and full with the wind and say that they resembled her own plump and fleshy belly that held her baby. Often, she would go into the town, her huge belly draped with flowing sheets of clothes, and bring me back special treats. But she was not an immortal fairy like we are. No, she was human, and like all humans, she could die. When her baby was born into the world, she died and was taken away from me; but as she died, I vowed that I would raise her child. For her sake, I have pledged to nurture this child, and I will not allow you to have this child.

Oberon: How long are you planning to stay in these woods?

Titania: Maybe until after Theseus's wedding. If you will be kind and patient, you can come along with us to celebrate the wedding; but if you will insist on behaving rudely and demanding that I hand over the boy, I will ask you to please leave. While we are in these woods together, I will stay away from your favorite places so that we do not have to see each other and run the risk of beginning another fight.

Oberon: Give me that boy, and I will happily stay with you for as long as you wish.

Titania: There is no way you can have this child. Come, all my fairies, we must leave now, because Oberon and I will have a terrible fight if we stay here for any longer.

Exit Titania with her fairies

Oberon: That is fine that you leave, Titania, but be warned that I will punish and humiliate you for not giving me what I want.

Close Reading Activities

First Read (Overview/First Impressions)

1. Distribute copies of *A Midsummer Night's Dream* Act II, Scene I (page 169) to students.

2. Have students number each paragraph in the passage in the left margin. Explain that they should refer to these numbers when quoting from the text.

3. Before reading, remind students that the first read is to help them gather their initial impressions of the text. Remind them to note the following on the text using the suggested marks:

   - questions about the text (?) (write question in the margin)

   - words or phrases they want to learn more about (put box around)

   - words or phrases that seem important (*)

   - areas of interest or confusion (!)

   - related ideas or concepts (⊂⊃) (write connection in the margin)

   - connections between sentences and paragraphs (◀—▶) (draw arrows connecting)

4. Have students read the text independently.

5. When they finish reading, ask them to revisit their notes and make additional annotations on the text.

6. Use a projector or document camera to display the text. Have students share their questions, thoughts, connections, and areas of confusion. Demonstrate how to record these ideas on the text.

Second Read (Figurative Language)

> **Preparation Note**
>
> On index cards, write the following examples of figurative language: "His hands were as cold as ice," "The stars are diamonds in the sky," "The leaves danced along the ground in the breeze," "My homework was a piece of cake," and "I'm starving to death!" On the board in five columns, write the types of figurative language: *simile, metaphor, personification, idiom,* and *hyperbole.*

1. Place students in five groups and give each group an index card. Have them place their index cards under the correct categories on the board. Discuss students' responses to review the types of figurative language.

2. Place students with partners. Have students read the text, with one student reading the part of Titania and the other reading the part of Oberon.

3. Have students underline the figurative language in the passage.

4. Display the text using a projector or document camera. Have students read the example of figurative language from the text. Underline the example on the projected text.

5. Discuss the example of figurative language with the class. Model for students how to make a note in the margin about the simile and how to explain its meaning.

6. Ask, "How does the comparison between Titania's friend's pregnant belly and ships' full sails help you better understand this portion of the drama?" (*gives a better understanding of the casual and very personal nature of the friendship, lets you see the friends' sense of humor and confidence, etc.*)

7. Distribute copies of the *Creating Comparisons* activity sheet (page 173) to students. Have students complete the activity sheet with partners.

8. When students have completed their activity sheets, ask them to share their answers as a class. Discuss how, when, and where authors use figurative language in literature.

Third Read (Connecting Information)

1. Display the text using a projector or document camera. Choose a volunteer to read Titania's first lines aloud.

2. Ask, "How do these lines develop the plot of this drama?" As students respond, remind them to support their answers with evidence from the text. Model how to take notes about it in the margins. Make sure students understand that Titania's lines provide background to help the reader understand her feelings about the boy and why she refuses to give him to Oberon.

3. Distribute copies of the *Text Connections* activity sheet (page 174) to students. Read the directions aloud.

4. Provide time for students to complete the activity sheet independently.

5. When students have completed the activity sheet, have students read their answers to a partner. Ask some students to share out to the whole class. Make sure students understand how Oberon's threat creates suspense by foreshadowing future danger to Titania.

Fourth Read (Applying and Analyzing Sources)

 **Preparation Note**

Locate a video clip of Act II, Scene I from the Internet, on DVD, or from a different media source.

1. Distribute copies of the *Similarities and Differences* activity sheet (page 175) to students. Tell them that they are going to watch a video clip of the same scene they just read. Explain that they should look for the similarities and differences between the two versions.

2. Show the video clip of Titania's opening lines. Then, stop the video.

3. Using a projector or document camera, project the *Similarities and Differences* activity sheet. Discuss the experiences of reading these lines and watching an actress perform them. Record students' ideas on the sample activity sheet. Then, have students add the ideas to their own sheets.

4. Refer to the description of Titania's friend's belly in the text and in the performance. Ask students to compare the two descriptions. Discuss how words have different effects depending on how they are delivered.

5. Play the rest of the video clip. Ask students to record other similarities and differences between the text and the performance.

6. Provide time for students to share their observations with the class. Record these on the projected activity sheet. Encourage students to add to their own notes.

Writing Connection

1. Review how the structure of a drama differs from other narrative forms. Discuss the benefits and challenges of relying on dialogue to convey feelings, emotions, actions, and themes.

2. Ask, "What did we learn about Oberon in the scene?" (*e.g., He wants the boy; He uses threats to get his way.*) Record students' ideas on the board. Point out that readers can learn many things from the dialogue.

3. Ask students to imagine what Oberon would say if he continued to speak at the end of the scene. Explain that the speech should expound on Oberon's feelings about Titania, the baby, and his situation. Students must use at least one example of figurative language.

4. Distribute copies of the *Shakespeare Reinvented* activity sheet (page 176) to students. Place students with partners to brainstorm ideas about what Oberon would say.

5. Give students time to complete the activity sheet independently.

6. Have students choose partners and practice reading their lines aloud. Provide time for them to make revisions.

7. Allow volunteers to perform their lines for the class live or via video recording.

Name: _____   **Date:** _____

Creating Comparisons

Directions: Read each phrase. Write a simile or metaphor to describe the characters' feelings.

Example: *Titania's feelings about the baby*

Titania protected the baby <u>like a fearless mother bear protects her cub</u>.

---

1. Titania's feelings about her dead friend

_____

_____

_____

_____

2. Titania's feelings about Oberon at the end of the passage

_____

_____

_____

_____

3. Oberon's feelings about Titania at the end of the passage

_____

_____

_____

_____

Name: _____ **Date:** _____

Text Connections

Directions: Reread the last sentence of the scene. Answer the questions. Support your answers with specific words and phrases from the text.

1. What emotions does Oberon's last line convey?

_____

_____

_____

_____

_____

_____

_____

_____

_____

2. How does Oberon's last line relate to the rest of the text passage?

_____

_____

_____

_____

_____

_____

_____

_____

_____

_____

_____

_____

Similarities and Differences

Directions: How are the text and the performance of the scene from *A Midsummer Night's Dream* similar? How are they different? Record your ideas on the Venn diagram.

Performance

Text

Name: _____ **Date:** _____

Shakespeare Reinvented

Directions: Write a speech for Oberon to give at the end of the scene from *A Midsummer Night's Dream*. In the dialogue, explain how Oberon feels about his situation. Include at least one example of figurative language.

_____

_____

_____

_____

_____

_____

_____

_____

_____

_____

_____

_____

_____

_____

_____

_____

_____

_____

_____

_____

_____

_____

_____

The Legend of Sleepy Hollow

Overview

The Legend of Sleepy Hollow provides an excellent opportunity to explore the development of setting in a story. In this lesson, students first ask questions, note unknown words and confusing phrases, and make connections with the text. In the second close reading activity, they differentiate between information that is presented explicitly, information that is inferred, and places where the text leaves matters uncertain. Next, students examine the development of the story's setting. In the final close reading activity, students study how particular words and phrases convey emotions and set the tone of the text. In the writing connection activity, students use the passage as a mentor text as they write their own descriptions of a familiar place.

Areas of Focus

- explicit vs. inferred information
- setting
- word choice
- describing the setting

Materials

- *The Legend of Sleepy Hollow* (page 178)
- *Information Sleuth* (page 182)
- *Setting Development* (page 183)
- *Setting the Tone* (page 184)
- *Setting the Scene* (page 185)
- projector or document camera

Standards

- Cite strong and thorough textual evidence to support analysis of what the text says explicitly as well as inferences drawn from the text, including determining where the text leaves matters uncertain.

- Analyze the impact of the author's choices regarding how to develop and relate elements of a story or drama.

- Determine the meaning of words and phrases as they are used in the text, including figurative and connotative meanings; analyze the impact of specific word choices on meaning and tone, including words with multiple meanings or language that is particularly fresh, engaging, or beautiful.

- Use precise words and phrases, telling details, and sensory language to convey a vivid picture of the experiences, events, setting, and/or characters.

The Legend of Sleepy Hollow

by Washington Irving

In the bosom of one of those spacious coves which indent the eastern shore of the Hudson, at that broad expansion of the river denominated by the ancient Dutch navigators the Tappan Zee, and where they always prudently shortened sail and implored the protection of St. Nicholas when they crossed, there lies a small market town or rural port. Some called it Greensburgh, but it is more generally and properly known by the name of Tarry Town. This name was given, we are told, in former days, by the good housewives of the adjacent country, from the inveterate propensity of their husbands to linger about the village tavern on market days. Be that as it may, I do not vouch for the fact, but merely advert to it, for the sake of being precise and authentic. Not far from this village, perhaps about two miles, there is a little valley or rather lap of land among high hills, which is one of the quietest places in the whole world. A small brook glides through it, with just murmur enough to lull one to repose. The occasional whistle of a quail or tapping of a woodpecker is almost the only sound that ever breaks in upon the uniform tranquility.

I recollect that, as a young man, my first exploit in squirrel-shooting was in a grove of tall walnut trees that shades one side of the valley. I had wandered into it at noontime, when all nature is peculiarly quiet, and was startled by the roar of my own gun, as it broke the Sabbath stillness around and was prolonged and reverberated by the angry echoes. If ever I should wish for a retreat where I might steal away from the world and its distractions, and dream quietly away the remnant of a troubled life, I know of none more promising than this little valley.

From the listless repose of the place, and the peculiar character of its inhabitants, who are descendants from the original Dutch settlers, this sequestered glen has long been known by the name of Sleepy Hollow. Its rustic lads are called the Sleepy Hollow Boys throughout all the neighboring country. A drowsy, dreamy influence seems to hang over the land, and to pervade the very atmosphere. Some say that the place was bewitched by a High German doctor, during the early days of the settlement. Others say that an old Indian chief, the prophet or wizard of his tribe, held his powwows there before the country was discovered by Master Hendrick Hudson. Certain it is, the place still continues under the sway of some witching power, which holds a spell over the minds of the good people, causing them to walk in a continual reverie. They are given to all kinds of marvelous beliefs, are subject to trances and visions, and frequently see strange sights, and hear music and voices in the air. The whole neighborhood abounds with local tales, haunted spots, and twilight superstitions; stars shoot and meteors glare oftener across the valley than in any other part of the country, and the nightmare seems to make it the favorite scene of her gambols.

Close Reading Activities

First Read (Overview/First Impressions)

1. Distribute copies of *The Legend of Sleepy Hollow* (page 178) to students.

2. Have students number each paragraph in the passage in the left margin. Explain that they should refer to these numbers when quoting from the text.

3. Before reading, remind students that the first read is to help them gather their initial impressions of the text. Remind them to note the following on the text using the suggested marks:

   - questions about the text (?) (write question in the margin)
   - words or phrases they want to learn more about (put box around)
   - words or phrases that seem important (*)
   - areas of interest or confusion (!)
   - related ideas or concepts (⬭⬭) (write connection in the margin)
   - connections between sentences and paragraphs (◄─►) (draw arrows connecting)
   - observations about the characters, plot, setting, etc. (underline)

4. Have students read the text independently.

5. When they finish reading, ask them to revisit their notes and make additional annotations on the text.

6. Use a projector or document camera to display the text. Invite students to discuss their questions, thoughts, and areas of confusion. Demonstrate how to record these ideas on the text.

Second Read (Explicit vs. Inferred Ideas)

1. To review the difference between explicitly stated information and implied information, write the following sentence on the board: *Devon stomped up the stairs to his room and slammed the door so hard that the house shook.* Ask, "What details are stated explicitly in this sentence?" (*Devon stomped upstairs; Devon went to his room; Devon slammed the door.*) Ask, "What can you infer from the sentence?" (*Devon is upset.*) Then ask, "What is left uncertain in this sentence?" (*Is he angry or sad? Is he in trouble? Did anything break?*)

2. Explain that it is important to differentiate between information that is presented explicitly, inferences made from the text, and places where the text leaves matters uncertain.

3. Distribute copies of the *Information Sleuth* activity sheet (page 182) to students. Display the activity sheet using a projector or document camera.

4. Ask a volunteer to read the first sentence of the text aloud. Model how to annotate the text to indicate which information is stated explicitly, implied, and uncertain.

5. Place students in six groups and assign each group one of the paragraphs in the text. Have each group read its paragraph closely to identify explicitly stated information, implied information, and areas of uncertainty. Ask students to record their findings on the activity sheets.

6. Provide time for groups to share their responses. Discuss how the author's choices affect the overall structure, tone, and meaning of the text.

Third Read (Setting)

1. Write the title of the text, *The Legend of Sleepy Hollow*, on the board. Ask, "What can you learn about the story from the title?" Discuss the implications of the word *legend* and the importance of the town name in the title. Make sure students understand how the title indicates the important role of the setting in the story.

2. Tell students that they will examine the development of the setting in the passage. Distribute copies of the *Setting Development* activity sheet (page 183) to students.

3. Display the text using a projector or document camera. Read the first paragraph aloud. Think aloud as you highlight details about the setting. Then, transfer the details to the activity sheet in the box for Paragraph #1.

4. Give students time to complete the activity sheet independently.

5. Place students in small groups to share their notes. Encourage students to add more details to their activity sheets.

Fourth Read (Word Choice)

1. Read this sentence aloud: "Not far from this village, perhaps about two miles, there is a little valley or rather lap of land among high hills, which is one of the quietest places in the whole world." Ask students to think about how this sentence makes them feel. Have them identify the specific words that created the feelings.

2. Distribute copies of the *Setting the Tone* activity sheet (page 184) to students. Project the activity sheet using a projector or document camera. Think aloud as you model how to fill in the chart.

3. Place students with partners to complete the activity sheet.

4. When students have completed the activity sheet, divide them into small groups to discuss their responses. Ask volunteers from each group to share out to the class.

5. Direct students' attention to the last sentence in the passage. Read it aloud. Ask, "How does this sentence relate to the overall tone of the passage?" Discuss the contrast between this statement and the previous description of Sleepy Hollow as a tranquil valley.

6. Guide students in a discussion about the tone of the text and how the author's word choices set the tone.

Writing Connection

1. Review the aspects of narrative text covered in the close reading activities (explicit vs. inferred ideas, setting, and word choice). Summarize how the author used these literary elements to describe the setting and set the tone.

2. Distribute copies of the *Setting the Scene* activity sheet (page 185) to students. Ask students to close their eyes and imagine a place they want to write about. The place can be real or imagined. Have them think about the things they see, smell, hear, feel, and taste in this place.

3. Tell students to open their eyes and quickly jot down notes about the sensory details in their setting. Have them add specific words and other telling details to their notes.

4. Give students time to write their setting descriptions.

5. When students have completed the writing assignment, place them in pairs for peer editing. Require students to give their partners one compliment and one suggestion for improvement.

Name: _____   **Date:** _____

Information Sleuth

Directions: Reread your assigned paragraph. Complete the chart below to indicate information that is stated explicitly, details that have to be inferred, and areas of uncertainty.

Paragraph #: _____

Explicitly Stated Information	Inferred Information	Areas of Uncertainty

#51505—*Connect to Text: Strategies for Close Reading and Writing*   © *Shell Education*

Name: _____ **Date:** _____

Setting Development

Directions: Read the text paragraph by paragraph. Record details about the setting from each paragraph. Then, explain how the author develops the setting over the course of the passage.

Paragraph #1

Paragraph #2

Paragraph #3

How does the author develop the setting over the course of the passage?

_____

_____

_____

_____

_____

_____

Name: _____ **Date:** _____

Setting the Tone

Directions: Choose five sentences in the text that contribute to the overall tone of the text. Copy the sentences on the chart below. Then, underline the words or phrases that have the strongest effect on the tone. In the second column, describe the words' effect on the tone of the story.

Sentence	Effect on Tone

Name: _____ **Date:** _____

Setting the Scene

Directions: Choose a real or imaginary place. Write a detailed description of the place. Include sensory details and precise words and phrases.

_____

_____

_____

_____

_____

_____

_____

_____

_____

_____

_____

_____

_____

_____

_____

_____

_____

_____

_____

_____

_____

_____

_____

References Cited

Brown, Sheila, and Lee Kappes. 2012. "Implementing the Common Core State Standards: A Primer on 'Close Reading of Text.'" Washington, DC: Aspen Institute. http://www.aspeninstitute.org/publications/implementing-common-core-state-standards-primer-close-reading-text.

Burke, Beth Anne. 2013. "Up Close with Close Reading." *Library Sparks* 11 (3): 14.

Conklin, Wendy, and Debby Murphy. 2014. *The How-To Guide for Integrating the Common Core in Language Arts.* Huntington Beach, CA: Shell Education.

Elder, Linda, and Richard Paul. 2014. "The Art of Close Reading: Part Three." Foundation for Critical Thinking. http://www.criticalthinking.org/pages/the-art-of-close-reading-part-three/511.

Fisher, Douglas, and Nancy Frey. 2014. *Close Reading and Writing from Sources.* Newark, DE: International Reading Association.

Fisher, Douglas, Nancy Frey, and Diane Lapp. 2012. "Close Reading in Elementary Schools." *The Reading Teacher* 66: 179–188.

Gallagher, Kelly. 2014. "Making the Most of Mentor Texts." *Educational Leadership* 71: 28–33.

Hathaway, Jessica. 2014. *TDQs: Strategies for Building Text-Dependent Questions.* Huntington Beach, CA: Shell Education.

Jones, Barbara, Sandy Chang, Margaret Heritage, and Glory Tobiason. 2014. "Supporting Students in Close Reading." The Center on Standards and Assessment Implementation. http://csai-online.org/sites/default/files/resource/38/Supporting%20Students%20in%20Close%20Reading.pdf.

Keir, June. 2009. *Argumentative Texts: Recognising and Creating Expositions, Responses and Discussions.* Greenwood, WA: Ready-Ed Publications.

Maloch, Beth, and Randy Bomer. 2013. "Informational Texts and the Common Core Standards: What Are We Talking About Anyway?" *Language Arts* 90 (3): 205–213.

McKeown, Margaret, Amy Crosson, Nancy Artz, Cheryl Sandora, and Isabel Beck. 2013. "In the Media: Expanding Students' Experience with Academic Vocabulary." *The Reading Teacher* 67: 45–53.

Morgan, Denise N., and Timothy V. Rasinski. 2012. "The Power and Potential of Primary Sources." *The Reading Teacher* 65: 584–594.

National Assessment Governing Board. 2007. *Writing Framework for the 2011 National Assessment of Educational Progress, pre-publication edition.* Iowa City, IA: ACT, Inc.

National Assessment Governing Board. 2008. *Reading Framework for the 2009 National Assessment of Educational Progress.* Washington, DC: US Government Printing Office.

National Governors Association (NGA) Center for Best Practices and Council of Chief State School Officers (CCSSO). 2010a. "Common Core State Standards." Washington,

DC: National Governors Association Center for Best Practices, Council of Chief State School Officers. www.corestandards.org.

National Governors Association (NGA) Center for Best Practices and Council of Chief State School Officers (CCSSO). 2010b. "About the Standards." Washington, DC: National Governors Association Center for Best Practices, Council of Chief State School Officers. http://www.corestandards.org/about-the-standards/.

Partnership for Assessment of Readiness for College and Careers (PARCC). 2015. *Structure of the Model Content Frameworks for ELA/Literacy.* http://www.parcconline.org/mcf/english-language-artsliteracy/structure-model-content-frameworks-elaliteracy.

Sisson, Diana, and Betsy Sisson. 2014. *Close Reading in Elementary School: Bringing Readers and Texts Together.* New York, NY: Routledge.

Snow, Catherine, and Catherine O'Connor. 2013. "Close Reading and Far-Reaching Classroom Discussion: Fostering a Vital Connection." Newark, DE: International Reading Association. http://www.reading.org/Libraries/lrp/ira-lrp-policy-brief--close-reading--13sept2013.pdf.

Veccia, Susan. 2004. *Uncovering Our History: Teaching with Primary Sources.* Chicago, IL: American Library Association.

Wilfong, Lori. 2013. *Vocabulary Strategies That Work: Do This—Not That!.* New York, NY: Routledge.

Answer Key

Feeling Proud (page 42)

Responses will vary. Students should draw an appropriate picture and write a sentence.

Helping Hand (page 43)

Pictures will vary. Students should draw an appropriate picture and label their drawing.

Kids Can Work (pages 44–45)

Responses will vary. Students should complete each sentence with a word or phrase describing how kids can work and how that work makes them feel. Students should draw appropriate pictures.

Saving and Spending (page 50)

1. The main idea of the text is to make choices about what you buy. You know this because the text says, "buying things is a choice."

2. Answers will vary. Sample answers include: The text says that buying things is necessary sometimes. It also says that you may buy things that you want. It is all a choice.

Picture Detectives (page 51)

1. Answers will vary. Sample answers include: The picture shows dolls at a store, and that is one item people might choose to spend money on. It is a want and not a need.

2. Answers will vary. Sample answers include: The picture shows people buying food at a store, and that is one item people might choose to spend money on. It is a need.

Money Choices (page 52)

Responses will vary. Students should write at least three sentences that describe the main idea of the text, which is that people make choices about what they buy. The text says, "buying things is a choice." The images show two choices that people might buy.

Students should draw an appropriate picture.

Ascending and Descending Order (page 58)

Responses will vary. Sample answers include: Ascending order and descending order are both ways to organize numbers, but the terms are opposites. The text says ascending order means "to list them from least to greatest." The text says that descending order means "to list them from greatest to least." The examples in the text support the idea that they are opposite ways to make a list of numbers.

Text Structure and Author's Purpose (page 59)

Responses will vary. Sample answers include:

Topic #1: Directions to get to a friend's house

Type of text structure: sequence/order

Why this text structure fits the purpose of the topic: It makes sense to put directions in sequential order because the reader would need to follow the steps in a specific order to get to the location.

Topic #2: Soccer vs. Baseball

Type of text structure: compare/contrast

Why this text structure fits the purpose of the topic: The vs. in the title indicates that these two subjects are to be pitted against one another with the goal of determining a "winner." Comparing and contrasting the merits and problems of the two sports would help the author prove his or her opinion about which sport is best.

Ranking Wealth (page 60)

1. Carlos Slim Helú
2. William Gates III
3. Warren Buffet
4. Mukesh Ambani
5. Lakshmi Mittal

Task Analysis (page 61)

Responses will vary. Sample answers include:

1. First, I referred back to the *Ordering Whole Numbers* text to double check the meaning of descending order. I verified that descending order means greatest to least.
2. Next, I read the whole list on the *Ranking Wealth* activity sheet.
3. Then, I went back and found the largest number on the list. I saw two people with $53,000,000,000. Then, I noticed that one of those two actually had $53,500,000,000. That person—Carlos Slim Helú—would be No. 1 on the list. The other person—William Gates III—would be the second.
4. Next, I went back to the list on the *Ranking Wealth* activity sheet to find the third largest number, which was $47,000,000,000. I added the person worth that amount—Warren Buffet—to the list in the third position.
5. Finally, I compared the last two numbers on the *Ranking Wealth* activity sheet list—$28,700,000,000 and $29,000,000,000—and determined that $29,000,000,000 was larger. That made Mukesh Ambani No. 4 and Lakshmi Mittal No. 5 on the list.

Traits of Hatshepsut (page 67)

Responses will vary. Sample answers include:

Caring—To make her father feel better about the loss of his sons, she sometimes wore boy's clothing.

Smart—She was intelligent; she was smarter than her husband.

Healthy—She was healthier than her husband.

Strong Leader—She made most of the decisions about the nation, and the priests and other leaders followed her advice.

Sentence Analysis (page 68)

1. The sentence tells more about Hatshepsut's family life, which is described in the paragraph.
2. The sentence also tells more about Hatshepsut's character and helps to tell the story of who she was and why she was an important figure in history, which is the goal of the passage.

Hatshepsut: Patient or Power-Hungry? (page 69)

1. The author's point of view is that Hatshepsut was a patient woman who waited many years before taking over the role she was born to fill.
2. Responses will vary, but may include the following pieces of evidence: This positive take on Hatshepsut's story is apparent in the author's word choices. For example, the author describes her original role by saying she was "only his (her husband's) regent." The author goes on to say she was smarter and healthier than her husband. The author also notes that she made most of the decisions, and "she was really the person who led Egypt through some of its best years." The author includes the detail that the next pharaoh, Thutmose III, "faded into the background at the palace" before Hatshepsut declared herself pharaoh.

Cause and Effect (page 70)

Causes	Effect
Hatshepsut is born into a royal family.	She had an important position in Egypt as daughter of the pharaoh and his first wife.
Hatshepsut's two brothers died young.	This left the royal family with no male heirs to follow their father into power.
Hatshepsut's father died when she was a teen.	There was no one else to take her father's place as ruler.
Hatshepsut learned to read and write and had learned to rule by watching her father.	Hatshepsut was intelligent and strong willed with ideas about how to make Egypt great.
Hatshepsut married her half-brother.	She became regent of Egypt and made most of the decisions for the country.
Hatshepsut's husband died while his son, Thutmose III, was just a baby.	Hatshepsut continued to rule the country as regent, making all the decisions and earning the people's respect.
Thutmose III faded into the background at the palace.	Hatshepsut was able to continue ruling Egypt as regent.
Hatshepsut declared herself pharaoh of Egypt.	Hatshepsut became the first female pharaoh in Egyptian history.

The Female Pharaoh (page 71)

Responses will vary. Students should include some of the causes and effects listed on the *Cause and Effect* activity sheet. They should include specific pieces of evidence, words, and phrases from the text.

Bill of Rights Summary (page 77)

Responses will vary. Students must summarize each amendment in their own words. Sample answers include:

1. The government cannot make laws about religions and it can't stop people from practicing their religion. The government cannot make laws that take away the freedom of speech, the press, the right of the people to gather peacefully, or the right to ask the government to fix its mistakes.

Inferences and Uncertainties (page 78)

Responses will vary. Sample answers include:

Amendment Number: I

Details Stated in the Text: Congress cannot make laws about religion or stop people from practicing their religion. Congress cannot make laws that take away the freedom of speech, or of the press, or the right of the people to peaceably assemble, and to petition the government for a redress of grievances.

Details Inferred from the Text: Americans have many freedoms protected by the First Amendment.

Areas of Uncertainty: Are there any limits to the freedom of speech, the press, or assembly? What if someone says something untrue about another person? What if a newspaper prints something untrue? What if people assemble and begin disturbing other people or property?

Analyzing the Bill of Rights (page 79)

Responses will vary. Students must include three themes in the Bill of Rights, such as fear of strong federal government, rights of individuals, importance of religious freedom, fairness for people accused of crimes, and strong state governments. Students must use evidence from the text to explain how the themes support a unifying purpose and how they conflict with that purpose.

Fact vs. Opinion (page 90)

1. Fact
2. Opinion
3. Fact
4. Fact
5. Opinion

Connecting Sentences (page 91)

(Owls are cool!)   Owls have three eyelids.

(Fire is scary.)   Fire is very hot.

Flowers bloom in spring.   (Spring is the best season.)

Lots of kids play soccer.   (Soccer is fun.)

(Plums taste better than candy.)   Plums are sweet and juicy.

My Perfect Job (page 92)

Responses will vary. Students must include a job and three reasons why they would like that job.

When I Grow Up… (page 93)

Responses will vary. Students must include a topic sentence that states an opinion about the best job and three reasons why they would like that job. They must also add a concluding sentence.

Questioning the Wish (page 99)

Responses will vary. Sample questions include:

1. How will you remember to give the guinea pig fresh water and food every single day?
2. How often will you clean the cage?
3. Who will care for the guinea pig on the nights you are busy with practices or homework?

Point of View (page 100)

Narrator's Point of View: I am ready for a pet.	"I believe I am ready to have my own pet. I am very responsible."
	"I am responsible and ready for the commitment!"
Parents' Point of View: You are not ready for a pet.	"My parents say I am not ready..."
Your Point of View: Responses will vary. You are probably ready for a pet. *or* You are not ready for a pet.	Responses will vary. Evidence that the author is ready for a pet: "I did some research at the library on guinea pigs." "I also went to the pet store to learn more about guinea pigs." "Every morning I get myself ready for school. I get dressed, brush my teeth and my hair, and pack my backpack. I know how to get myself breakfast and rinse my dishes when I am done. I also help take care of my little brother. I walk him to school in the mornings and pick him up after school. I help him tie his shoes and button his jacket." Evidence that the author is NOT ready for a pet: "My parents say I am not ready..." "Pets can be a lot of work."

Paragraph Structure (page 101)

Why did the author write paragraph #1? The author wrote paragraph #1 to state the position that he/she wants a guinea pig for a pet and that he/she is ready for the responsibility.

Why did the author write paragraph #2? The author wrote paragraph #2 to state the position that he/she wants a short-haired guinea pig.

Why did the author write paragraph #3? The author wrote paragraph #3 to support the position that he/she is prepared to care for the guinea pig.

Why did the author write paragraph #4? The author wrote paragraph #4 to support the position that he/she is responsible enough to care for a pet.

Why did the author write paragraph #5? The author wrote paragraph #5 to restate the position that he/she wants a guinea pig and is responsible enough to care for it.

Organizing an Opinion (page 102)

Responses will vary. Students must write an opinion statement expressing a birthday wish. They must write three supporting arguments. They must write a conclusion statement reiterating their birthday wish.

My Birthday Wish (page 103)

Responses will vary. Students will write an essay including an opinion statement expressing a birthday wish, three supporting arguments, and a conclusion statement reiterating their birthday wish.

Comparing Calendars (page 109)

Arguments Against the Traditional School Calendar	Arguments in Support of the Year-Round School Calendar
Summer vacation is too long. Most people do not live on farms, so it is unnecessary to take a summer break. Traditional schedule is hard for working families.	Vacations are spread throughout the year. Having one month off in summer still allows kids to go to summer camp. Students and teachers would feel less burned out during the school year because vacations would be spread out. Some students show improvement with year-round schools.

School Calendars (page 110)

1. 3; June, July, August
2. 3; March, July, November
3. Responses will vary. A sample answer is: The chart helps me see that the school year is equal in length, but with a different vacation schedule. I see how the breaks in year-round school are spaced throughout the year.

Opinions and Reasons (page 111)

Paragraph 1 Main Argument: Summer vacation is too long.	**Reasons:** Students forget what they learned over the summer. They have to spend time reviewing what they already learned every fall. They have to readjust to school schedule every fall.
Paragraph 2 Main Argument: The traditional school schedule was made for farm families.	**Reasons:** Students no longer need summers off to help with farm harvests. Most people no longer live on farms.
Paragraph 3 Main Argument: The traditional school schedule is hard for working families.	**Reasons:** Working parents do not get summer vacations, so they have to find child care. The change in schedule, which happens twice a year, is disruptive to families. Change is hard for families.

Paragraph 4 Main Argument:	Reasons:
The year-round school calendar is better for students and families.	Students are in school the same amount of time, but vacations are spaced throughout the year.
	Students could still go to summer camp.
	Students and teachers would not be as burned out with vacations spaced throughout the year.
Paragraph 5 Main Argument:	**Reasons:**
Research is not clear on which school calendar is better, but the author thinks year-round school is best.	Some students show improvement.
	Other students do not show improvement.

Outline of an Opinion (page 112)

Responses will vary. Sample opinions and reasons are:

1. Opinion #1: Having school in the summer is too expensive for schools.

Reasons: It is expensive to cool school buildings in summer months. Homeowners pay the highest electricity bills in the summer months, and schools would have to do the same.

2. Opinion #2: Children need the downtime that summer vacation provides.

Reasons: Children should be spending time outside when the summer weather is warm and sunny. Children need fresh air and exercise for healthy development.

3. Opinion #3: Summer vacation is an American tradition.

Reasons: American children have always had summers off. Summer vacation is part of growing up in America. Everyone looks forward to summer vacation.

Siding with Tradition (page 113)

Responses will vary. Students must compose an opinion in support of the traditional school schedule. The opinion piece must have a clearly stated position, three opinions, two to three reasons to support each opinion, and a clear concluding statement, as well as at least three transition words or phrases.

Objective and Subjective Summaries (page 119)

Responses will vary. Students must rewrite the subjective summary as an objective summary by removing all opinion statements from the text.

Language Decoder (page 120)

Responses will vary. Sample answers are:

Sentence from Text	Literal Meaning	Figurative Meaning
The US National Park System is a treasure that must be preserved.	The lands are treasures (jewels and gold).	The US National Park System contains lands that are very important to our country and should be taken care of.
They are oases where we can relax and view wildlife in its own element.	The parks are places with water and trees in the middle of a desert.	The parklands are special locations around the country in the midst of ordinary highways, cities, towns, and other development, where people can enjoy nature.
A glut of tourists chokes the parks with cars that cause pollution and run over wildlife.	Tourists are actually choking, as in using hands to strangle, parks.	Tourists drive cars into parks, which cause air pollution and endanger animals.

National Park Claims and Evidence (page 121)

Responses will vary. Sample answers are:

Claim	Evidence
National Parks are some of the few places in the United States where wildlife is protected.	The land is covered with cities and factories, and the amount of green space shrinks all the time. Parks preserve lands and animals. Parks show people what life was like long ago.
The National Parks are in danger.	People's cars bring pollution to the park and endanger animals. People's campfires cause wildfires. People's motorboats harm and scare animals and pollute the water. Snowmobiles bring noise and pollution to parks and scare animals.
The National Park Service must limit tourism.	They should limit the number of cars allowed in parks. Allow fewer snowmobiles or ban them. Forbid motorboats near coastal parks. Even though some people will be outraged at first, they will like the results of these limits.
Selling parklands is even worse than allowing tourism.	Parklands have been sold to developers. Houses might soon be built in some parks.
Another danger to the parks is oil drilling.	Public lands could be opened to oil drilling. Oil drilling can damage the ecosystems.

Response Research (page 122)

Responses will vary. Students must have a central argument with at least four supporting reasons. The reasons must have supporting evidence.

National Parks Preservation Response (page 123)

Responses will vary. Students' opinion pieces must have a central argument, supporting reasons, and evidence to support the reasons.

Introduction Analysis (page 129)

1. Wilson was giving the speech on Flag Day. He referred to where the flag had been and where it would go as he explained his decision to enter WWI. The flag is a symbol of unity, power, and the national purpose, according to Wilson. Emphasizing American unity was important in this speech, as he wanted all Americans to unite behind his decision to enter the war.

2. Responses will vary. Wilson asked the questions rhetorically to make his listeners consider their own responses as he spoke.

Flag Day Claims and Evidence (page 130)

1. Claim: The actions of the German government forced the US into the war.

Reason or Evidence: Germany insulted America and took aggressive action against the country. America has to defend its dignity and freedom.

2. Claim: German military leaders denied America the right to be neutral.

Reason or Evidence: Germany sent spies and conspirators to America. These spies and conspirators tried to change the minds of Americans by spreading sedition. They used violence to destroy American industries and disrupt the nation's economy. They tried to get Mexico to fight America and Japan to join Mexico in that fight.

3. Claim: Americans and the German people are not enemies.

Reason or Evidence: The German people did not start this war. They did not wish that America would be drawn into the war. America is fighting the cause of the German people, as well as our own cause. The German people are being controlled by a "sinister power."

Historical Analysis (page 131)

1. Wilson's objective was to rally the support of the American people for his decision to enter World War I. Wilson used strong language to prove that war was America's only option. For example, "The extraordinary insults and aggressions of the Imperial German Government left us no self-respecting choice but to take up arms in defense of our rights as a free people and of our honor as a sovereign Government." He added that Germany "denied us the right to be neutral."

2. Wilson answered his own question within the question. He was stating what he believed to be the obvious answer. He said that America was sending soldiers overseas for the "old, familiar, heroic purpose for which it has seen men, its own men, die on every battlefield upon which Americans have borne arms since the Revolution."

3. Wilson is reminding Americans of every battle in American history, including the American Revolution and the Civil War. He referenced the Revolution by name, which serves as a reminder that America exists because young men were willing to fight and die to win the nation's freedom from England.

4. Wilson lays blame on Germany's "military masters" to define the problem as a fight against the "sinister power" that controls Germany. He goes on to say that America and the German people are not enemies. He says that Americans are fighting for the cause of the German people, as well as for our own cause. This was an important distinction to make because America was a nation of immigrants, many of them German immigrants. In order to rally the support of the American people—including its many German immigrants—Wilson had to specify that it was at war with the German government and not the German people.

Building an Argument (page 132)

Responses will vary. Students should state a claim, support it with three reasons, define the opposing argument, make a counterargument, and state a conclusion.

War Decisions (page 133)

Responses will vary. Students should compose an argument that states a claim, provide three reasons in support of the claim, define the opposing argument, make a counterargument, and state a conclusion.

Beach Question (page 144)

Responses will vary. Students must write one question about the text. A sample question is, "Did they swim?"

Rhyming Word Pairs (page 145)

dog—log; hat—cat; pig—wig; sun—bun; net—jet

Beach Picture (page 146)

Responses will vary. Students must draw an appropriate picture.

My Favorite Place (page 147)

Responses will vary. Students must draw an appropriate picture and write about the place.

Story Summary (page 153)

Responses will vary. A sample response is:

Paragraph #: 1
Key Words: question, night, day
Summary: The animals must decide whether to have night all the time or day all the time.

The central message of the story is that perseverance pays off, which means we should never give up. I know this because the chipmunk stayed awake all night and chanted his vote of light and then night. His perseverance paid off because the legend says that ever since that night when the chipmunk called so long and loud for "light and night," there has been both day and night.

Character Analysis (page 154)

Responses will vary. Sample answers include:

Bear	Chipmunk
big voice	wide-awake
strong-willed	never gave up
kept working for a long time	confident
bad-tempered	cheery
angry	spry
clumsy	good-humored

1. Bear and chipmunk both chanted their opinions longer than the other animals.

2. Bear gave up, but chipmunk persevered. Bear is clumsy, while chipmunk is spry. Finally, bear has a bad temper, but chipmunk is cheery and just laughs when bear tries to get him.

3. Chipmunk has perseverance. He chanted all night long, after all the other animals gave up and went to sleep.

Character Point of View (page 155)

Responses will vary. Sample answers include:

> Bear's Point of View: Bear wants it to be night all the time.
>
> How do I know? He chanted, "Night, night! Always night!"
>
> Chipmunk's Point of View: Chipmunk wants day and night.
>
> How do I know? He chanted, "We will have light—and then night. We will have light—and then night!"

Perseverance Story Planner (page 156)

1. Responses will vary. Students must choose a story that shows perseverance in their own lives. They must note the first, next, and last events that happened.

2. Responses will vary. Students must tell what they learned and how they felt about it.

I Can Persevere (page 157)

Responses will vary. Students must compose a personal narrative about perseverance.

Pirate Inferences (page 164)

Question	Text Says...	Inference	I Know...
How does Captain Butterbeard feel about the "cruel-looking crewman"?	"I don't have to tell ye mates that we stand to make a small fortune on this haul, but we have to work together!" The captain stopped suddenly and stared directly into the eyes of a particularly cruel-looking crewman.	The Captain does not trust the man.	I know that when someone stares a person down, they are singling them out and trying to drive their point home to that person in particular.
Was Captain Butterbeard pleased with the crew's reaction to his plan?	Captain Butterbeard allowed himself a cautious smile. There would be no mutiny today!	Yes, he was pleased.	When a person smiles, it means he or she is pleased. Also, I know that a captain does not want a mutiny; the fact that "There would be no mutiny today!" would have been good news for the captain.

Figurative Language (page 165)

1. acrobat—bird; simile; The acrobat did a graceful move high in the air.

2. he—vacuum cleaner; simile; The boy ate quickly.

3. you—sunshine; metaphor; You make my day brighter and happier.

4. she—cheetah; simile; She is a fast runner.

5. legs—rubber; metaphor; His legs felt shaky and weak because he was nervous.

Do Pirates Have Feelings? (page 166)

Responses will vary. Sample answers include:

Feeling	Text Evidence
suspicious	Captain Butterbeard looked suspiciously at his crew. Which one of them would betray him?
pleased	The crew operated like a pack of wolves. The strongest one would lead until he was challenged successfully by an underling. Captain Butterbeard liked that about them.
hopeful	"By tomorrow morning, her cargo will be stowed in our hold, and her crew will be secured in our brig, ready to ransom!"
confident	The captain strutted confidently in front of the assembled crew.

I Address My Crew (page 167)

Responses will vary. Sample answers include: I eyed my crew suspiciously. Which of these scurvy dogs will betray me? I picked each one of these miserable rats myself. My crew is the foulest, rudest, most deadly lot in the sea! They can rob, pillage, and loot better than any other crew, but I wouldn't trust them with my worst enemy's wooden leg! They are a pack of wolves, they are! I must never show weakness, or they will challenge my power. Lucky for me, I have no weakness!

Creating Comparisons (page 173)

Responses will vary. Sample answers include:

1. Titania's friend was more precious to her than jewels.
2. Titania's anger at Oberon is reaching a boiling point.
3. Oberon was confident he could swat Titania down like an annoying fly.

Text Connections (page 174)

Responses will vary. Sample answers include:

1. Oberon was annoyed that Titania would not give him what he wanted, but he was confident that he would get back at her. He ended their conversation with a threat, "That is fine that you leave, Titania, but be warned that I will punish and humiliate you for not giving me what I want."

2. Oberon was referring to Titania's refusal to give him the boy. We know, from the beginning of the passage, that the boy was the son of Titania's dear friend. Titania refused to give up the boy because she had promised her friend she would care for him. Titania refused to break her promise, which irritated Oberon and prompted him to make the threat.

Similarities and Differences (page 175)

Responses will vary.

Shakespeare Reinvented (page 176)

Responses will vary. Students must continue Oberon's dialogue and express his feelings about the situation. They must include at least one example of figurative language.

Information Sleuth (page 182)

Responses will vary. Sample answers include:

Paragraph #: 2

Explicitly Stated Information	Inferred Information	Areas of Uncertainty
tall walnut-trees that shade one side of the valley Sabbath stillness If ever I should wish for a retreat where I might steal away from the world and its distractions, and dream quietly away the remnant of a troubled life, I know of none more promising than this little valley.	This valley is a beautiful, quiet, and peaceful place. The narrator has strong, positive feelings about this place.	What does the narrator mean by, "dream quietly away the remnant of a troubled life"? Did the narrator have a troubled life? Or was he referring to someone else who had a troubled life and hid away in that valley? Does the narrator still live in this place?

Setting Development (page 183)

Responses will vary. Sample answers include:

Paragraph 1: small market town or rural port; Not far from this village, perhaps about two miles, there is a little valley or rather lap of land among high hills, which is one of the quietest places in the whole world; A small brook glides through it, with just murmur enough to lull one to repose; The occasional whistle of a quail or tapping of a woodpecker is almost the only sound that ever breaks in upon the uniform tranquility.

Paragraph 2: grove of tall walnut-trees that shades one side of the valley; If ever I should wish for a retreat where I might steal away from the world and its distractions, and dream quietly away the remnant of a troubled life, I know of none more promising than this little valley.

Paragraph 3: listless repose of the place; sequestered glen has long been known by the name of Sleepy Hollow; A drowsy, dreamy influence seems to hang over the land; bewitched; an old Indian chief, the prophet or wizard of his tribe, held his powwows there; under the sway of some witching power, which holds a spell over the minds of the good people, causing them to walk in a continual reverie; They are given to all kinds of marvelous beliefs, are subject to trances and visions, and frequently see strange sights, and hear music and voices in the air; The whole neighborhood abounds with local tales, haunted spots, and twilight superstitions; stars shoot and meteors glare oftener across the valley than in any other part of the country, and the nightmare seems to make it the favorite scene of her gambols.

How does the author develop the setting over the course of the passage?

Responses will vary. Sample answers include: The author began with pleasant descriptions of the peaceful valley. He introduced the idea of violence by describing the shot he fired into the stillness. In the third paragraph, the peace of the valley becomes more sinister as he describes the mysterious feeling in the area. He adds details about bewitching, spells, trances, visions, haunted spots, superstitions, etc. Finally, he ends by saying that, "the nightmare seems to make it the favorite scene of her gambols." By the end, the reader has a sense that this peaceful valley is shrouded in mystery and danger.

Setting the Tone (page 184)

Responses will vary. Sample answers include:

Sentence	Effect on Tone
A small brook <u>glides</u> through it, with just <u>murmur</u> enough to lull one to <u>repose</u>.	Paints a picture that is peaceful, sleepy, and idyllic.
I had wandered into it at noontime, when all nature is peculiarly quiet, and was startled by the <u>roar</u> of my own gun, as it broke the <u>Sabbath stillness</u> around and was prolonged and reverberated by the <u>angry echoes</u>.	This sentence marks a change in tone from peaceful to mysterious. It suddenly introduces danger and anger into the setting.

Setting the Scene (page 185)

Responses will vary. Students will write a detailed description of a place that includes sensory details and precise words and phrases.

Reading Level Chart

Page	Text Title	Lexile Level	GR	DRA	Reading Recovery	Early Intervention
39	I Can Work	BR*	A	1	A, B	1
47	Choices	390L	H	14	13–14	13–14
54	Ordering Whole Numbers	710L	Q	38	NA	27
63	Hatshepsut: The Female Pharaoh	860L	U	50	NA	28
73	The United States Bill of Rights	1590L	NA	NA	NA	NA
86	The Best Job	40L	A	1	A, B	1
95	The Birthday Wish	630L	O	34	27–28	25
105	Let's Have Year-Round School	710L	Q	38	NA	27
115	Saving Our National Parks	1010L	Y	60	NA	32
125	Flag Day Address June 14, 1917	1250L	NA	NA	NA	NA
140	At the Beach	NP*	NA	NA	NA	NA
149	Why the Chipmunk Has Black Stripes	610L	O	34	27–28	25
159	Captain Butterbeard Addresses His Crew	770L	S	40	NA	27
169	A Midsummer Night's Dream Act II, Scene I	1170L	NA	NA	NA	NA
178	The Legend of Sleepy Hollow	1620L	NA	NA	NA	NA

*Beginning Reading

*Non Prose

Contents of the Digital Resource CD

Page(s)	Title	Filename
16	Standards	standards.pdf
28	Text Structure Chart	textstructure.pdf
39	I Can Work	work.pdf
42	Feeling Proud	proud.pdf proud.docx
43	Helping Hand	helpinghand.pdf helpinghand.docx
44–45	Kids Can Work	kidscanwork.pdf kidscanwork.docx
47	Choices	choices.pdf
50	Saving and Spending	saving.pdf saving.docx
51	Picture Detectives	picture.pdf picture.docx
52	Money Choices	moneychoices.pdf moneychoices.docx
54	Ordering Whole Numbers	orderingnumbers.pdf
58	Ascending and Descending Order	order.pdf order.docx
59	Text Structure and Author's Purpose	structure.pdf structure.docx
60	Ranking Wealth	wealth.pdf wealth.docx
61	Task Analysis	taskanalysis.pdf taskanalysis.docx
63	Hatshepsut: The Female Pharaoh	hatshepsut.pdf
67	Traits of Hatshepsut	traits.pdf traits.docx
68	Sentence Analysis	analysis.pdf analysis.docx
69	Hatshepsut: Patient or Power-Hungry?	patientorpower.pdf patientorpower.docx
70	Cause and Effect	effect.pdf effect.docx

Page(s)	Title	Filename
71	The Female Pharaoh	pharaoh.pdf pharaoh.docx
73	The United States Bill of Rights	billofrights.pdf
77	Bill of Rights Summary	summary.pdf summary.docx
78	Inferences and Uncertainties	inference.pdf inference.docx
79	Analyzing the Bill of Rights	analyzingbill.pdf analyzingbill.docx
86	The Best Job	bestjob.pdf
90	Fact vs. Opinion	opinion.pdf opinion.docx
91	Connecting Sentences	connecting.pdf connecting.docx
92	My Perfect Job	perfectjob.pdf perfectjob.docx
93	When I Grow Up...	grow.pdf grow.docx
95	The Birthday Wish	birthday.pdf
99	Questioning the Wish	questioning.pdf questioning.docx
100	Point of View	pointofview.pdf pointofview.docx
101	Paragraph Structure	paragraph.pdf paragraph.docx
102	Organizing an Opinion	organizing.pdf organizing.docx
103	My Birthday Wish	mybirthday.pdf mybirthday.docx
105	Let's Have Year-Round School	school.pdf
109	Comparing Calendars	comparing.pdf comparing.docx
110	School Calendars	calendars.pdf calendars.docx
111	Opinions and Reasons	reasons.pdf reasons.docx

Page(s)	Title	Filename
112	Outline of an Opinion	outline.pdf outline.docx
113	Siding with Tradition	tradition.pdf tradition.docx
115	Saving Our National Parks	parks.pdf
119	Objective and Subjective Summaries	objective.pdf objective.docx
120	Language Decoder	langdecoder.pdf langdecoder.docx
121	National Park Claims and Evidence	parkclaims.pdf parkclaims.docx
122	Response Research	research.pdf research.docx
123	National Parks Preservation Response	response.pdf response.docx
125	Flag Day Address June 14, 1917	flagday.pdf
129	Introduction Analysis	introduction.pdf introduction.docx
130	Flag Day Claims and Evidence	flagdayclaims.pdf flagdayclaims.docx
131	Historical Analysis	historical.pdf historical.docx
132	Building an Argument	building.pdf building.docx
133	War Decisions	wardecisions.pdf wardecisions.docx
140	At the Beach	thebeach.pdf
144	Beach Question	beachq.pdf beachq.docx
145	Rhyming Word Pairs	rhyming.pdf
146	Beach Picture	beachpic.pdf beachpic.docx
147	My Favorite Place	favorite.pdf favorite.docx
149	Why the Chipmunk Has Black Stripes	chipmunk.pdf
153	Story Summary	story.pdf story.docx

Page(s)	Title	Filename
154	Character Analysis	character.pdf character.docx
155	Character Point of View	characterview.pdf characterview.docx
156	Perseverance Story Planner	storyplanner.pdf storyplanner.docx
157	I Can Persevere	persevere.pdf persevere.docx
159	Captain Butterbeard Addresses His Crew	butterbeard.pdf
164	Pirate Inferences	inferences.pdf inferences.docx
165	Figurative Language	language.pdf language.docx
166	Do Pirates Have Feelings?	piratefeel.pdf piratefeel.docx
167	I Address My Crew	mycrew.pdf mycrew.docx
169	A Midsummer Night's Dream Act II, Scene I	dream.pdf
173	Creating Comparisons	comparisons.pdf comparisons.docx
174	Text Connections	textconnect.pdf textconnect.docx
175	Similarities and Differences	differences.pdf differences.docx
176	Shakespeare Reinvented	reinvented.pdf reinvented.docx
178	The Legend of Sleepy Hollow	sleepyhollow.pdf
182	Information Sleuth	sleuth.pdf sleuth.docx
183	Setting Development	setting.pdf setting.docx
184	Setting the Tone	tone.pdf tone.docx
185	Setting the Scene	scene.pdf scene.docx

Notes

#51505—Connect to Text: Strategies for Close Reading and Writing